THE
BATTLEFIELDS
OF BRITAIN

THE
BATTLEFIELDS
OF BRITAIN
John Kinross

DAVID & CHARLES
Newton Abbot   London

HIPPOCRENE BOOKS, INC
New York

For the late
Private C. Kinross VC
49th Battalion,
Canadian Expeditionary Force 1918
Born Uxbridge, Middlesex 1896
Died Lougheed, Alberta 1957

British Library Cataloguing in Publication Data

Kinross, John
   The battlefields of Britain.
   1. Battles - Great Britain -
   History
   I. Title
   914.1
   ISBN 0-7153-7679-9

Published in the United States of America by

Hippocrene Books
171 Madison Avenue
New York, N. Y. 10016

Library of Congress Catalog Card Number 79 84233
ISBN 0 88254 4837

Typeset by Ronset Limited, Darwen,
Lancashire
printed in Great Britain
by Biddles Limited, Guildford
for David & Charles (Publishers) Limited
Brunel House Newton Abbot Devon

Contents

Introduction

Battlefields in Britain are rather dull. Today there may, if you are lucky, be a cross and a guidebook in the local church but only those with imagination can really picture the scene on the day of action—smoke, noise, confusion and courage—the former three preventing the fourth from being seen. In Scotland the work of the National Trust for Scotland has turned Bannockburn, Auldearn, Culloden Moor and Killiecrankie into tourist spots and the action is made realistic by dioramas and recorded commentaries. Only at Bosworth Field have the English anything comparable. I am not suggesting that we necessarily want to turn all battlesites into tourist areas but more could be done at Halidon Hill, St Albans and countless other battlefields where there is not even a cross or battle plaque.

This book is an attempt to help the battle enthusiast—be he schoolboy or pensioner—to discover what is worth seeing. No one should miss the splendours of Bosworth, but the brass plate in Sutton Cheney church is often ignored. Similarly at Killiecrankie the tourist may go away with a photograph of the car park and road kiosk, when the actual battlefield monument in the most peaceful of sylvan settings is some distance away on the other side of the road.

Respect for private property should be considered of course, and it is polite to write a note in advance to see monuments at Evesham, Stoke or the one mentioned above at Killiecrankie.

What has prompted the choice of the battles included in this book? Some of the early actions—Pilleth, Harlaw, Ashdown—have been omitted because their sites are uncertain or their details largely guesswork. In the Civil War there were many small actions like those at Winceby, Nantwich, Chalgrove and Rowton Heath that I have omitted because there is a limit to space and because they are of less importance than those included. The first battle of Newbury has been omitted, although it was a fairly large affair, as it was disorganised and followed no set pattern.

This book does not attempt to be a history of warfare, but it is interesting to note the change in weapons and battle formations during the years. In Norman times the battleaxe was used by foot soldiers to great effect. The only armour was a helmet and archers used short arrows which they fired into the air rather than straight at the enemy. The English bow came into its own at Halidon Hill with devastating effect. Less than twenty years before the Welsh archers had suffered badly at Bannockburn, being unprotected from the advancing Scots. After this the English were careful to keep horse available on the flanks to protect their archers. The longbow was the most effective weapon for many years on the Continent and throughout the Wars of the Roses.

There was a change at Pinkie, an action which saw the use of guns on a large scale—arquebusiers from Spain and ships' cannon from Clifton's fleet. No English soldier took kindly to innovation however. Henry V had a master of ordinance—Nicholas Merbury—but his bombards were used mostly for siege work and it was his archers who won fame at Agincourt. After Pinkie the arquebus or its German equivalent, the hackbut, was fairly common and as late as 1557 an Act of Parliament decreed that persons in Wales, Lancashire and Cheshire—the latter county being famous for its bowmen—should provide and keep a hackbut or, in lieu, a longbow and sheaf of arrows. It was partly the lack of practice that made the bowmen obsolete rather than the accuracy of the handgun.

Cavalry tactics are generally supposed to have been brought in by Prince Rupert during the Civil Wars. In the Wars of the Roses the heavy knights crashed their way through with lances and battleaxes, usually fighting the knights on the other side. Those best armed went in front, a tactic used by the Scots at Flodden, and weight was relied on for effect. Speed was not essential. Rupert's innovation, based on the experience he had gained with Gustavus Adolphus, was vastly different from the old idea of the 'caracole' in which the horse trotted up to the enemy, fired their pistols in line, then withdrew to make way for the second line. Rupert taught his men to charge through the enemy using their swords and pistols at close range. By this means he could break the enemy ranks and chase them off the field. Sometimes musketeers followed up his charge to clear up the remaining enemy. The trouble with these tactics was the complete absence of Rupert and his cavalry at crucial moments in the action. Cromwell carried out a similar tactic but was careful not to leave the field. He was the first commander—Dunbar and Worcester are perhaps his finest achievements in open battles—to actually take in what every unit was doing and to rush reinforcements to where they were needed, when they were needed. The Royalists often lost battles from having split commands and the Scots at Dunbar suffered from having too many preachers and 'old decayed serving-men and tapsters' as Cromwell described the Parliamentary riff-raff that fought at Edgehill.

The civilians suffered little in the Wars of the Roses, where they were spectators rather than participators, but in the Civil War sieges were cruel to all persons. Poor Joan Butt of Gloucester petitioned Governor Massey during the siege that she was unable to pay her dues, having twenty soldiers to look after and only two milk heifers. She had her mare sequestered for her pains.

Much has been written about the arms and combatants of the '45 in the section dealing with their battles. Before this, however, the British army was reorganised. One of the men responsible was William Blathwayt, Secretary-at-War from 1683 to 1717. Personally accompanying William III in his Flanders campaign, Blathwayt saw at first hand the necessity for providing proper military stores. William first created the English field army that performed so miraculously under John Churchill, Duke of Marlborough, who owed his first appointment to the unfortunate James II. One of the most unlucky commanders was surely the Earl of Feversham, whose army melted away in 1688 when William landed at Torbay and he was forced to flee the country like his master James, while the fortunate Churchill changed sides without any apparent difficulty or loss to his future career.

What happened to the old soldiers? During the Civil War some managed to successfully petition for pensions. Captain Floyd, who served in Colonel Charles Gerrard's Regiment of Foot, was wounded at Cheriton by a musket shot in the middle of the back. He lay in pain for some weeks, with half-a-week's pay and the cost of physicians to meet and was entirely dependent on friends for his survival. He sent a petition to Charles I at Oxford and was awarded £20 for his pains, a sum which was considerable for those days. After the Restoration Charles II allocated £60,000 for indigent officers and Chelsea Hospital was built for old soldiers, still surviving for that purpose today. Perhaps it is comforting to note that the National Army Museum is its neighbour today.

The final action in this book is Fishguard, where a collection of fencibles, seamen and Pembroke Yeomanry outwitted a larger band of French revolutionary soldiers, armed to the teeth with the most up-to-date muskets and ammunition in sufficient quantity for a siege. The Frenchmen were mostly gaolbirds who refused to fight, were untrained and had no motivation. Soldiers must be trained to use their arms to the best advantage: they are useless as untrained, ill-armed men. One could never really doubt the outcome of Sedgemoor. As Field Marshal Montgomery wrote in 1946: 'The most important single factor in war is morale. It is impossible to prosecute a war for long if the will of the people to fight is lacking; in such a case the national war machine will not function. In battle it is morale which counts and no strategy can succeed without it. Once morale has gone, defeat is inevitable.'

Acknowledgements

Thanks are due to the Librarian of the Royal Military College, Sandhurst, where most of this book was written, to the staff of the National Army Museum and the Wallace Collection, London, for their help with the photographs. Special help has been obtained from Sir Donald Cameron of Lochiel on the '45, from Major Naesmyth of Posso RA on Stoke and Newark, on the Battle of Wakefield from the Wakefield Historical Society, from the National Trust of Scotland on some of the Scottish battles, the Leicestershire County Council on Bosworth Field and Mr D. G. Alcock of The Almonry Museum, Evesham on the Evesham engagement.

Finally I must thank my family for their patience and my publishers for their invaluable advice and for producing this book in the first place.

J.S.K.
Steventon,
Hampshire
1979

Ethandun/878AD

The White Horse at Westbury; Bratton Camp is on the top of the hill (*author*)

England seemed a doomed kingdom in the year 871. Northumbria was occupied by the Norsemen, Mercia by both Danes and Anglo-Saxons but in Wessex, at least that part to the west of Southampton Water, a semblance of order was maintained by King Ethelred. This king—not to be confused with his better-known namesake 'The Unready' who ruled a hundred years later—had already beaten the Danish invaders of King Guthrum at Ashdown, which is generally considered to be on the Ridgeway near Lowbury Hill as the Danes were driven back to their camp at Reading.

When Ethelred died, however, his brother Alfred took over the kingdom and the Danes took fresh heart. In 876 a Danish force entered Dorset and captured Wareham. Alfred moved up and surrounded the town but the Danes broke out and made for Exeter where they were safe behind the walls. The remaining force in Wareham left by sea but were destroyed in a storm off Swanage. Alfred moved back to his base at Chippenham and held

King Alfred's statue in Winchester (*The Winchester Stamp Centre*)

a great feast to celebrate Twelfth Night; the Danes, now regrouped, attacked in the middle of the feast and scattered Alfred's men. Alfred and a few thegns escaped to the Isle of Athelney in Somerset and lived like beggars for the rest of the winter; many of their colleagues went to France. Alfred waited until the weather improved, then sent our messengers for a general assembly of local fyrds or militias to a place called 'Ecgbryghts stane', a standing stone near Brixton Deverill. Meanwhile a Danish fleet under Ubba entered the River Parrett, at Combwich, where there was a ford, the fleet was becalmed, Alfred descended on it and by weight of numbers defeated the Danes, capturing their famous Raven banner.

The Battle

The Danes under Guthrum at Chippenham set off to meet Alfred's force, which was reinforced by men from Hampshire at Eastleigh Wood on the River Wylye. Guthrum's men reached Edington and Alfred, according to the *Anglo-Saxon Chronicle*, 'fought against all the Army in a dense, shield-locked array, and long maintaining a stubborn fight, and at length by Divine Will obtained a victory and overthrew the pagans with the greatest slaughter, and striking down the fugitives,

followed them as far as their stronghold'. For fourteen days Alfred besieged Chippenham and the hunger and cold forced Guthrum to surrender.

The Peace of Wedmore followed and there was a baptismal ceremony at Aller. Guthrum was the first to be baptised.

The Site

Edington village is just off the B3098 between Westbury and Urchfont; Bratton Down is above it nearer Westbury and Edington Hill. The battle might have taken place at either of these places. The tradition that Westbury White Horse was carved to celebrate the battle is not based on fact. Alfred, advancing on Chippenham, would more likely have occupied Tinhead Hill and Edington Hill, as the Danish camp could be viewed from these points.

There is another Edington near Sedgemoor on the Polden Hills but this, although near Athelney, would not be near enough to Chippenham and there is no record in the *Chronicle* of the Danes having another headquarters. The London Museum has some Danish axes which would be similar to those used by Guthrum's men. Alfred's troops relied on their shield wall for pushing down the advancing Danes and then finished them off with spear and sword.

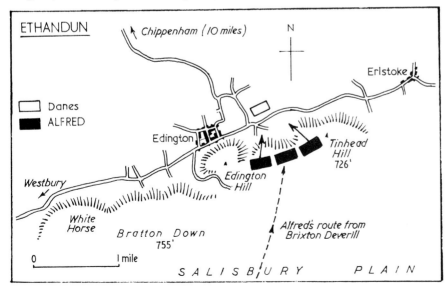

Stamford Bridge/25 September 1066

The Battle of Stamford Bridge has always been overshadowed by Hastings, yet it was equally important in its way. Harold's brother Tostig, Earl of Northumberland, joined forces with King Hardrada of Norway and was determined to regain his Earldom, for he had been banished by his brother for failing to look after the north and his land and title given to Morcar; he also had his eye on the English throne. Tostig caused trouble as far south as the Isle of Wight but Harold chased him round to the Humber, where he lost some ships and men to Morcar and Harold's fleet, and was forced to take refuge in Scotland. The combined army of Morcar and Edwin (Harold's two brothers-in-law) was defeated by the Vikings of Hardrada and Tostig's men, many of whom were Scottish levies, at Fulford outside York in mid-September. The Vikings had sailed up the Ouse from the Humber and left their boats at Riccall. For some reason they did not advance on York after Fulford, although they had no news of

Harold's approach. Instead of trying to make a camp in York they went to the east and camped on the River Derwent at Stamford Bridge. By 24 September Harold with his 3,000 men was in Tadcaster and the following day he entered

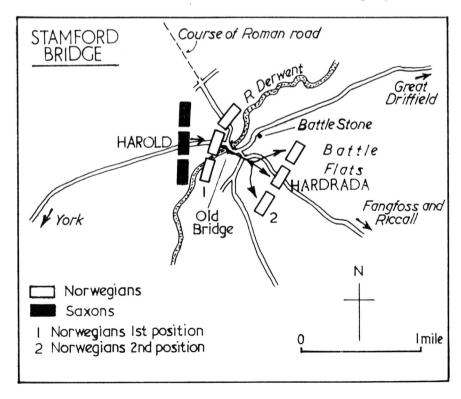

STAMFORD BRIDGE

Course of Roman road

R Derwent

Great Driffield

Battle Stone

HAROLD

Battle Flats

HARDRADA

York

Old Bridge

1

2

Fangfoss and Riccall

N

☐ Norwegians
■ Saxons
1 Norwegians 1st position
2 Norwegians 2nd position

0   1 mile

York where he was strengthened by the remnants of Edwin and Morcar's army. Harold was never one to waste time and as soon as he had realised the Viking army was on the Derwent, eight miles east o York, he decided to attack them there.

The Battle

Harold Hardrada was an experienced soldier. He had left his fleet under Olaf and about 1,000 men at Riccall, so his force was only marginally larger than Harold's army—say 4,000 to 5,000. He had taken no precuations against a sudden attack. Even when the English vanguard arrived he left part of his army where it was on the west (ie York) bank, drawing up his main force in the Battle Flats on the east bank. The Derwent was 40 feet wide and its banks very slippery. The only bridge, some 500 yards upstream from the present one, was undamaged. Harold quickly reached it, defeating the small and unco-ordinated force on the west bank. However the bridge was defended by a well armed Viking wielding an axe, who is said to have killed 50 men, before a local man jumped into a swill tub in the river and pushed a sword through the planks of the bridge, stabbing him in the leg. The vanguard of Harold's army, mostly archers, rushed over and quickly deployed, shooting down the Vikings at close range. Hardrada was killed. Tostig regrouped his men and was offered his life by Harold but refused it. Tostig had expected reinforcements from Olaf, but when they arrived it was too late; Tostig was dead, supposedly killed by his own brother, and Olaf was allowed to withdraw with a mere 20 ships on the promise that he would never invade England again. Harold had won a great victory but at a terrible cost and his real battle was yet to come. Had there been no Stamford Bridge, Hastings might have been a different story.

The Battlefield Today

The village of Stamford Bridge on the A166 is now busy with traffic and there is little to see. There is a battle stone on the green by the mill with the inscription 'SLAGET VED STAMFORD BRUBLE UTKJEMPET IDISSE TRAKTER DEN 25 SEPTEMBER 1066' in Norwegian and the English translation: 'The Battle of Stamford Bridge was fought in this neighbourhood on September 25, 1066'. Battle Flats is still marked on the map and there is a local field of the same name. At Stillingfleet Church near Selby some iron-work on the old doorway resembling Viking ships is supposed to commemorate the battle.

The battle stone on the green near Stamford Bridge (*author*)

The monument to King Harold at Battle (*The British Tourist Authority*)

The victory for Harold at Stamford Bridge was costly. Not only were many of his leaders killed or wounded, but all his men were exhausted. William and his army of 10,000 landed at Pevensey two days later. His army was well equipped and his claim to the English throne was as strong as Harold's, for he was a cousin of Edward the Confessor and a direct relation of King Canute, whose wife Emma had been his great aunt. Harold was Edward's brother-in-law but had been chosen king by the Witan.

The Normans had mailed armour made of iron rings and pointed helmets with protective nosebars. Their cavalry was also well armed: their horses had steel frontlets and high saddles. Their archers had small arrows and short bows (some very small arrows can be seen in the London Museum). William's banner had been blessed by Pope Alexander and his men were optimistic of victory.

Harold stopped in London to gather more troops. His faithful housecarls fought with two-handed swords and long-handled axes. Some carried javelins and their long shields protected them when held together in a shield wall. Harold's cavalry was few in number and inferior to the Norman's, but his archers had more powerful bows and he had some ballista and stone-throwing engines. His levies—most of them unarmoured and untrained—were equipped with clubs, knives and pitchforks.

The Battle

Harold positioned his army in a long line with the centre where Battle Abbey now stands. He had about 7,000 men, and reinforcements arrived during the battle. In the centre he placed himself and the two banners of the Wessex Dragon and the Fighting Man; he had the height advantage over William, whose army approached from Telham Hill, where he deployed his

The death of Harold (*Radio Times Hulton Picture Library*)

men in three divisions. Count Alan of
Brittany and his men were on the left,
archers in front, then infantry then horse,
William himself in the centre and his
Flemings and French under Eustace of
Boulogne on the right. The Norman
arrows made no impression on the shield
wall and a mass of javelins and rocks
drove back the Normans. The Bretons on
the left wing retreated in disorder as far
as the Asten Brook where William, who
had lost his horse, is reported to have said
'Look at me well. I am still alive and by
the Grace of God I shall yet prove victor';
he cut off the pursuit and brought forward
his knights. The shield wall did not
flinch. William, recalling his success with
the Bretons, tried a ruse. He ordered them
to flee once more and they succeeded in
bringing Harold's right wing with them,
which was cut down by the heavily armed
knights. William now reached the 'hoary
apple tree' hill and made a flank attack
on Harold. His archers were ordered to
fire high over the shield wall. One arrow
struck Harold in the eye just as twilight
was setting in. The shield wall gave way
and the battle was over. Some of Eustace's
men following up fell down a ravine
known as the Malfosse, where the housecarls turned on them and killed them.

William returned to Hastings, where he

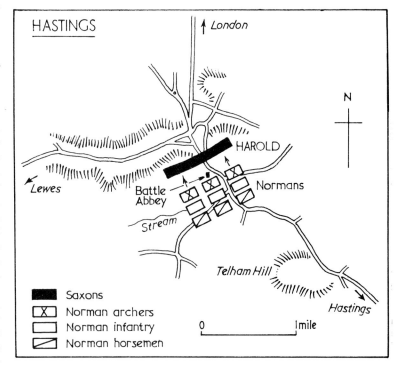

buried Harold by the seashore. His army
reached Berkhamsted via Wallingford in
seven weeks and there the Londoners
came out to offer him the crown.

Results

No other battle fought in England was as
important as Hastings. In place of the ill-
disciplined Saxon rule came the Norman
iron fist. William brought feudalism and
strong government to the country and
internationally he consolidated the West
at a time when Islam was conquering the
East.

The Battlefield Today

Battle Abbey, which is open to the public,
is on the A2100 from Hastings. The com-
memoration stone is supposed to mark the
spot where Harold fell. There is a farm
track leading off the B2095 that provides
a good viewpoint. An axehead was found
in Marley Lane but no other relics have
been discovered.

The Standard/22 August 1138

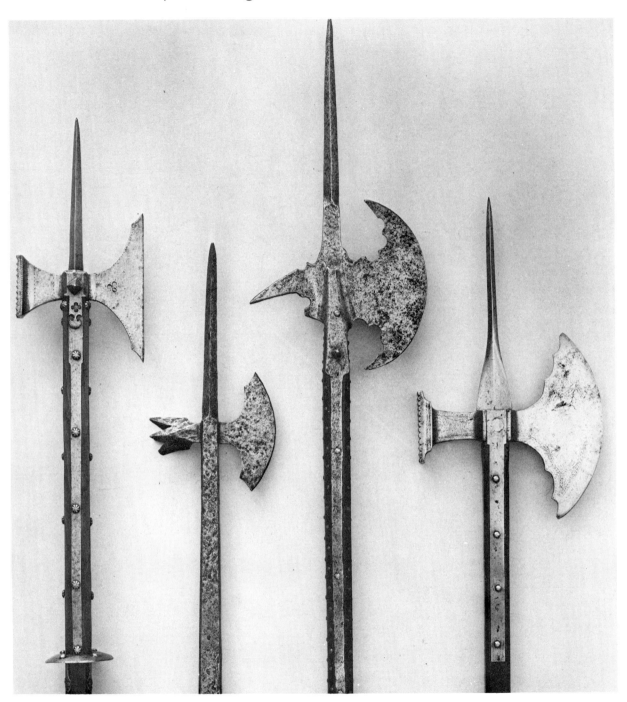

Poleaxes—the type of weapon used at The Standard (*Reproduced by permission of the Trustees of the Wallace Collection*)

King Stephen inherited a troubled country in 1135. His cousin Matilda had an equal claim to the throne and she was supported by King David I of Scotland. He also claimed part of Northumberland as his wife's property and on these two counts led an army into England. It was huge in size, sometimes reported as 22,000, but

16

probably about half that number. Many of David's soldiers were fierce warriors from Galway. Others were French and even English mercenaries. They plundered as they went and in Hexham the women were bound in ropes and taken to Scotland.

Stephen was in no position to come to the aid of his northern counties. In Bristol, Robert, Earl of Gloucester, was in revolt and the Constable of Dover supported him, making it unsafe for Stephen to move north. However old Thurstan, Archbishop of York, summoned an army in York to march under his standard, an enormous mast tipped by a silver pyx hung with the banners of St Peter of York, St John of Beverley and St Wilfred of Ripon. Two of his supporters were Bruce and Balliol, men well known in Scotland, who tried to arrange a truce with young Prince Henry of Scotland. The Archbishop's commanders, Walter Espec of Helmsley, Gilbert de Lacy and William le Gros, Earl of Albemarle, led their army to Cowton Moor, near Northallerton. The English left their horses and baggage near Northallerton Castle (now no longer

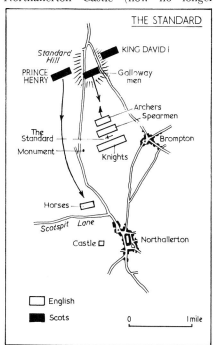

visible) in Scotspit Lane. William le Gros was the builder of Scarborough Castle, possibly financed by a grateful English crown in reward for his services.

The Scots army, with Prince Henry and most of the mounted knights on the right wing, the Galloway warriors in the centre and the King on the left, were positioned on Oaktree Hill (now called Standard Hill) and opposite them Espec placed the archers in front, then the spearmen and finally the knights behind. Strangely most of the knights seem to have fought on foot. This may have been as an example to their men, or perhaps because they were not afraid of the few Scots who were on horseback.

The Battle

The Scots' wild charge was checked by the English archers, and the Galwegians looked 'like a hedgehog with quills' according to the Abbot of Rievaulx who was present. The scratch English army fought bravely, though outnumbered. The Galwegians finally gave way and Prince Henry, seeing a hole appear in the English centre, suddenly charged down on their horses and baggage. The English third line saved the day by turning and encircling the Prince's men. The Danes and Normans in David's army fought fiercely and many were killed. Suddenly panic struck the Scots and they retreated; Henry and his father reached Carlisle but thousands were left dead on the field, mostly in Scotspit Lane and mainly Scots. The English lost de Lacy and perhaps a hundred men.

The Standard Today

Leave Northallerton on the A167 and the monument is easily found three miles north on to the right of the road. On the field of battle is appropriately a football field. By the hospital is Scotspit Lane, a heavily wooded sunken lane where some bones and metal remains were found about a hundred years ago.

The Standard monument (*author*)

17

Lewes/14 May 1264

The Baron's War between King Henry III and his principal nobles was really a long struggle to control the government of the country. The provisions of Simon de Montfort's 'mad Parliament' in Oxford of 1258 were ignored by Henry, who was backed by King Louis of France. Most of the King's strength was in Wales, the North and the Midlands; Simon's strength lay in London and the South. In early May 1264 the King arrived at Lewes having successfully relieved Rochester Castle and captured Tonbridge. Simon was recruiting in London. He had a mere 5,000 men, dressed in Crusade-style uniform with white crosses, and Bishop John of Chichester blessed them on the field; Simon was determined to have God on his side. He placed his left wing of Londoners under Nicholas Seagrave near some chalkpits on the hill above Offham. His right wing commanded by his sons Guy and Henry was near the present racecourse grandstand. In the centre was Gloucester's division and he himself commanded the most experienced troops in the reserve.

De Warenne, formerly one of Simon's men, had declared Lewes Castle for the King, which probably accounted for Simon's haste to do battle with him. Prince Edward was in the Castle with a picked group of knights and horsemen, the King was in St Pancras Priory and Richard, the King's brother, known as the 'King of the Romans' as he had once tried to claim the Imperial throne, commanded the left wing in the forthcoming battle.

The Battle

Unlike other battles, Lewes was fought in stages. The young Edward was some way away from the King and as soon as he realised that the rebel army was drawn up, he gathered his men and set off for the hill to the London side of the town to attack the London contingent, who had recently insulted his mother, threatening to drown her as a witch. Edward's knights soon dispersed the Londoners, some of whom fled back home. Others were trampled on by the horses or fell down the hill. Edward followed the main body north and was out of the rest of the battle.

In the meantime the King and his brother had positioned themselves in two groups at the foot of the hill and realised that they had to advance to meet Simon as they had lost touch with Edward. The two sons, Henry and Guy, beat back the 'King of the Romans', who was cut off from his men and captured in a windmill. Simon and Gloucester attacked the King who 'was much beaten with swords and

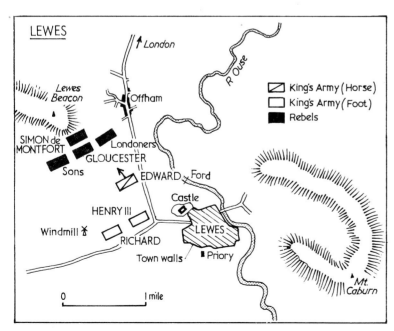

LEWES

↑ London

R. Ouse

Lewes Beacon

Offham

	King's Army (Horse)
	King's Army (Foot)
■	Rebels

SIMON de MONTFORT

Londoners

GLOUCESTER

Sons

EDWARD Ford

Castle

HENRY III

LEWES

Windmill ☀

RICHARD

Town walls

■ Priory

Mt. Caburn

0   1 mile

18

maces, and, two horses killed under him, escaped with difficulty'. In just two hours the battle was over and the King had retreated to his Priory.

Meanwhile Edward returned and attacked Simon's baggage train, unknowingly killing some royal prisoners. He got through to the Priory but lost most of his knights on the way.

Results

Simon had won a great victory by defeating his enemy piecemeal. If Edward had fought with his uncle and father, the result might have been different. In 1810 some 1,500 skeletons were found in a pit near the modern gaol, and although Simon lost many men, including William Blund his standard bearer, most of the bones were of royal soldiers. The King was now a prisoner in Simon's hands. Edward was sent to Hereford and Richard to Kenilworth. It was for the setting up of the first parliament of knights from the shires and two representatives from each of the chartered boroughs that Lewes was famous.

The Battlefield Today

There is little to see of the battlefield at Lewes. The castle remains are interesting **Lewes Castle**

though, with a museum in the gatehouse. The direction of Edward's attack must have been difficult for horses with heavily armed riders. On the top of Harry's Hill is a monument. There are no remains of the windmill and virtually no trace of the Priory.

19

Evesham/4 August 1265

The Archbishop of Canterbury conducts the service of dedication of the Simon de Montfort memorial, made from stone from the de Montfort Castle ruins in France (*Cheltenham Newspaper Co Ltd*)

Prince Edward escaped from his guards in May 1265 at Hereford and made off to Wigmore Castle. Soon he had collected an army at Worcester, and prominent in it were the Duke of Gloucester and Roger Mortimer, previous allies of Simon de Montfort. Simon's son, young Simon, was besieging Pevensey Castle in Sussex when summoned by his father to join forces. King Henry was still Simon de

Montfort's prisoner at Hereford. By the end of July, young Simon, after attacking Winchester, had arrived at Kenilworth with an army slightly larger than that of his father. He appears to have been in no hurry to join up with his father and probably thought it wiser to remain at Kenilworth, which was easier to defend than Hereford. It was surrounded by a moat with only one drawbridge. Nevertheless the rebel leaders preferred to billet in more comfort in the town and priory.

Edward decided to prevent old Simon from joining his son and moved on Evesham, which he assumed would be the natural stopping place between Hereford and Kenilworth. First, however, he moved on Kenilworth and in the early hours of 1 August he attacked young Simon's troops outside the castle and routed them, capturing many horses, banners and supplies. Young Simon escaped by swimming the moat. On 2 August old Simon, unaware of his son's defeat, crossed the River Severn at Kempsey, south of Worcester, and entered Evesham. Here he was protected by the loop of the Avon and there was but one bridge at Bengeworth on the London road that offered a

20

line of escape if an enemy arrived from the north. Edward approached Evesham in three columns; Mortimer's detachment peeled off at Cleeve Prior and made for Bengeworth; his own and Gloucester's detachments made for Offenham and crossed there, presumably by ferry though there may have been a bridge there in 1265, with their captured banners in front so that Simon's scouts would think they were the army of young Simon.

The Battle

When he at last realised he was trapped— an enterprising barber climbed the abbey tower and spotted Mortimer blocking the Bengeworth bridge—Simon is supposed to have said 'Let us commend our soul to God, because our bodies are theirs'. The few horse in front, then the English foot and finally the Welsh spearmen were arranged in a tight group and Simon planned to break out between Gloucester and Edward. The weather—the battle was fought in a thunderstorm—was on his side. Edward, however, perched on Green Hill, could see the approaching rebels clearly in spite of the weather. His line sagged on Simon's attack but his wings spread out and surrounded the smaller army. Many of the Welsh deserted and were drowned attempting to cross the river. The English horse and foot in Simon's army fought for two hours and they were cut down in hundreds. Simon himself was killed and his son Guy wounded. Henry III, in armour on the battlefield, was only just recognised in time or he too would have been killed. Many tried to escape towards Offenham and there is a place by the river known as Dead Men's Ait, where many perished. Bones were dug up there in the eighteenth century, so it might have been a burial ground. Edward had won a resounding victory. The war dragged on until Kenilworth finally surrendered in December 1267 due to shortage of supplies.

The Battlefield Today

There is a monument in the grounds of

Abbey Manor, which is private. It states that 'The Earl with his eldest son Henry de Montfort, 18 barons, 160 knights and 4,000 soldiers were slain in the battle'. This is not the battle site which is in the field below, where there is a well, or more accurately a piece of wet ground near a market garden. It is best approached by a track at the top of Green Hill Road.

In the Abbey grounds a block commemorates Simon's grave. It was recently erected (1965) and unveiled by the Speaker of the Commons and dedicated by the Archbishop of Canterbury to the founder of the English Parliament.

King Henry in danger at Evesham (*Radio Times Hulton Picture Library*)

21

Bannockburn/24 June 1314

The death of Sir Humphry Bohun

The victory at Falkirk over Wallace by King Edward I tightened the English grip on Scotland and in August 1305 Sir John Menteith, Governor of Dumbarton, captured Wallace and sent him to London for trial. The Scots looked round for a new leader. In 1306 Bruce disposed of the Balliol claimant, John Comyn, and had himself crowned as King of Scotland. He was excommunicated by the Pope and a great number of Scots were opposed to him because of his murder of Comyn. Bruce with about 200 men was defeated at Perth by the Earl of Pembroke and went into hiding in Ireland.

The death of Edward I in 1307 and the accession of the weak and ineffectual Edward II was the real spur to Scottish hopes. In 1314 a large English army arrived in Edinburgh of about 22,000 men, including some of Bruce's Scottish opponents. It set off to relieve Stirling Castle which Bruce's brother was besieging. The castle governor, Mowbray, had agreed to hand it over by Midsummer Day unless relieved by an English army.

Bruce's Scottish army consisted of about 8,000 men. He had 5,000 spearmen in three squadrons commanded by his brother, Douglas and Moray. His horse were a mere 500 under Sir Robert Keith, but they were lighter and faster than the English horse, which were heavily armed

and weighed down with impedimenta. The Welsh bowmen were the main threat to Bruce's small army but he chose his site for the battle well—there was a Royal Park near St Ninians on the Bannock burn that was unfavourable to cavalry. He made sure that his camp in a wood was well protected by pits covered by sticks and turf and by wicked calthrops, so that the English horse would not bear down on him in a sudden attack.

Like Waterloo, Bannockburn had its preliminary battle. Edward sent Lord Clifford, Sir Thomas Gray and 300 horse to attempt to break through to Stirling Castle. They were blocked by Randolph Moray's spearmen who captured Gray. The Scots formed a schiltron and beat back the English knights who, seeing more Scots approaching, withdrew to the main body on the banks of the marshy Bannock. Meanwhile Sir Humphry Bohun, one of Gloucester's vanguard, saw Robert Bruce emerge from the wood ahead of his army. He spurred his horse forward and levelled his lance trying to settle the affair for his King by himself. The age of chivalry was still present. Bruce rose in his stirrups and brought down his battle-axe on the rash knight, shattering both axe and helmet with one mighty blow. The Scottish army needed no finer encouragement.

The Battle

Bannockburn was a battle fought over a whole day. The Scottish schiltrons of

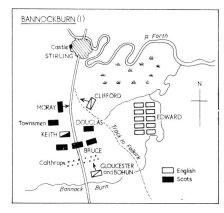

Douglas and Walter the Steward were on the left wing, Randolph Moray in the centre and Edward Bruce on the right. Robert Bruce commanded the reserve and the cavalry of Keith was positioned behind with instructions to cut down the Welsh archers if possible. The English van under Gloucester bore down on Edward Bruce and the muddy ground made progress difficult. King Edward sent his archers round to the right wing to pour in a flank attack on Douglas. The moment Keith's horse had been waiting for arrived and they charged down in a circling gallop on the unfortunate archers who had no supporting pikes. The Scottish archers took heart and dashing in between the schiltrons poured their arrows at close range into the English ranks. Edward was still confident of his overwhelming weight of numbers, but looking up on Gillies' Hill he saw a large body of flag waving men about to descend on his flank. This was too much and he spurred forward to get through to Stirling with a handful of his knights. One of them, Sir Giles d'Argentan, refused to escape and dashed his horse into the nearest schiltron with the taunt: 'I am not accustomed to fly, nor shall I do so now'. They were his last words.

The Stirling townsmen now came into the action. It was they who had been spotted waving blankets on Gillies' Hill and, armed with knives and clubs, they finished off the wounded and fleeing English soldiers. The King at Stirling was advised by Mowbray to make for the border and with 500 knights he escaped, closely followed by Douglas with 60 horse. At Dunbar he shipped to Berwick. Seven hundred knights were killed, many like Grey were taken prisoner and only one body commanded by Lord Pembroke, and containing the remnants of the Welsh archers, made orderly retreat to Carlisle. Bruce was generous to his enemies. He received Mowbray in his camp with honour and allowed many to return home unransomed like the gallant Sir Marmaduke Twenge who had fought nobly at Stirling Bridge, and surrendered himself to Bruce the following day after lying hidden in a wood. A Stirling wheelwright named Kinross was given property in the town for his efforts—reputedly he was the last to arrive at the battle.

Conclusion

The Scottish Declaration of Arbroath was an attempt to clear themselves from the wrath of the Pope. They argued that from time immemorial Scotland had been a free country until Edward I 'in the guise of friend and ally' had made himself tyrant and oppressor. The Scots pledged to recognise Bruce as their King as long as he resisted England, and as long as there were a hundred Scots left to fight for freedom. It was a bold statement and perhaps history will recall it today. There were other battles won by Bruce's men, like Myton-on-Swale, in Yorkshire, and the capture of Berwick before Edward agreed to a truce in 1323 that lasted for 13 years.

The Battlefield Today

Bannockburn is a few miles south of Stirling on the A80. Part of the site is protected by the National Trust for Scotland and there is a centre with an audio-visual display of the battle. The English-made statue of the Bruce on his charger weighs three-and-a-half tons and was unveiled by the Queen in 1964. The Bruce wore a special crown attached to his helmet so that he could be recognised by his men. This was how Humphry Bohun also recognised him.

The statue of King Robert the Bruce at Bannockburn (*The National Trust for Scotland*)

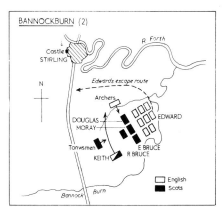

Halidon Hill/19 July 1333

The Scottish charge

Not to be confused with Homildon Hill, the Battle of Halidon Hill near Berwick was a lesson by Edward III for the Scots to respect his claimant to their throne, Edward Balliol. The latter had been crowned at Scone in 1332, but was turned out of Scotland by his enemies, Sir Archibald Douglas and the Earl of Moray, who placed young Robert the Steward on the throne as regent while overtures were made to David in France. Edward ignored the Treaty of Northampton, whereby he had promised to recognise Scotland as a free and independent kingdom, and marched on Berwick, which was held by Sir Alexander Seaton. The latter agreed to surrender by 11 July, provided he was not relieved before that date. Sir William Keith managed to get a small force into Berwick while another party of Scots burnt Tweedmouth. There was a further agreement between Edward and Keith, who took over from Seaton as Governor, to surrender on 19 July unless relieved by 200 men. Meanwhile Douglas's army moved to Dunspark, near Halidon Hill and Edward, seeing the Scots banners, moved his army in three divisions to the top of Halidon Hill, commanding the approach to Berwick from the north.

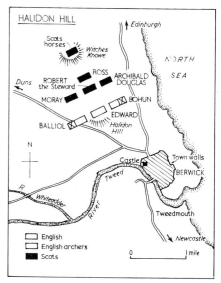

The Battle

Halidon Hill, according to legend, started with a personal duel between Turnbull, a Scottish knight, and Sir Robert Benhale of Norfolk. After a great struggle observed by the two armies Benhale won, and the Scots gave the word to advance, their grooms taking their horses to the rear. Also in the rear was Lord Ross with a hand-picked force of Scottish knights. The English archers waited until the Scots were on the boggy area below Halidon before opening a devastating fire. The Scots tried again and again to turn the English off the hill but they failed. Douglas was speared and captured. Ross, fighting bravely against Balliol, was also slain. The Scots were hampered in their retreat because the grooms had vanished with the horses. Many were killed by the English knights in the pursuit all the way to Ayton. The English losses were only the Newcastle men who arrived late and, according to records, one knight.

The Battlefield Today

Halidon Hill is easily found from Berwick. Take the A6105 and two miles before Duns, near the maternity home, is the hill. A rough cairn marks the battle site and there is an ordnance survey pointer on the crest of the hill.

The walls and castle remains of Berwick are well worth visiting.

Neville's Cross/17 October 1346

In August 1346 Edward III's army in France had a great victory over King Philip at Crecy. The French called on their allies, the Scots, to invade and give France a bit of breathing space. However, as at the time of the Standard (*see* p 16), the King had made satisfactory arrangements for the Church to look after the defence of the northern counties during his absence. The Archbishop of York collected an army at York, which included men under the Bishop of Carlisle, Lord Neville of Raby Castle, Lord Percy and

their adherents. King David II of Scotland with Robert the Steward and Douglas entered England via the Esk valley. They were delayed by a veteran soldier, Thomas Selby, at Liddel Castle, which took them several days to capture. Selby was killed and the Scots, some 20,000 strong, camped at Bearpark, outside Durham.

The Battle

Lord Neville, in command of the English army, now advanced and caught the Scottish vanguard at Sunderland bridge, and pushed them back. He deployed his army on Red Hill, overlooking Durham (roughly along the line of the railway), with Rokeby and the Archbishop on the left and Percy on the right. Each division was preceded by archers, then foot, then horse. The Scots at Bearpark had Douglas on the right, the King in the centre and Robert on the left. They were first stung into action by the English archers and, abandoning their positions on the hill, attacked all along the line. The English archers noticed that Douglas and the King's divisions had to narrow their front at one stage to avoid a ravine and many were killed here. Percy and Neville were pushed back but Lord Lucy, commanding the rearguard, came up at the crucial moment, like Norfolk's men at Towton, and the Scots gave way. The King was captured crossing the River Browney and the advance of Rokeby and Percy now finished the battle.

King Edward III in France was delighted with the news of his northern army's success. He had just won Poitiers and King David was later ransomed for 100,000 marks in 1358 on condition the Scots broke their French alliance. King John of France, Edward's other captive, was forced to make a similar agreement and some considerable portion of Northern France became English property. The dealings of Edward after Neville's Cross and Poitiers could have taught Charles I a few lessons about what to do with his prisoners after Lostwithiel (*see* p 78).

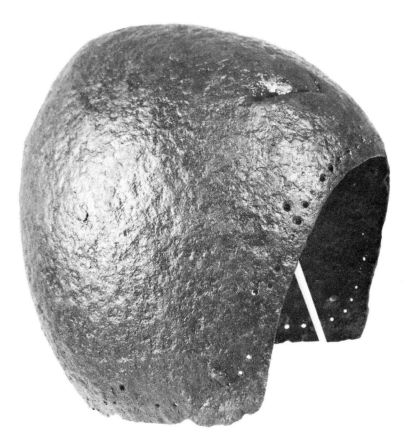

A fourteenth-century bascinet
(*Glasgow Art Gallery and Museum*)

The Battlefield Today

The battlefield is much built up today. The ravine can be seen near Neville's Cross roundabout on the A1. Take Toll House Road off the A1 and turn left to Baxter's Wood. There is a stump of the original cross remaining near the roundabout, but the original monument was apparently destroyed in the sixteenth century. Perhaps it is now time to repair it.

A longsword, 1350–1400
(*Glasgow Art Gallery and Museum*)

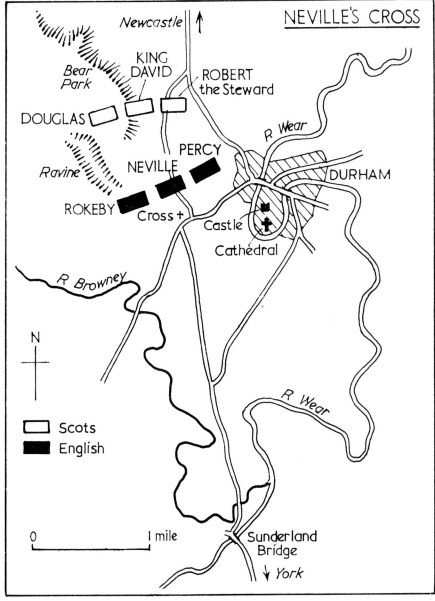

NEVILLE'S CROSS

Newcastle

Bear Park

KING DAVID

ROBERT the Steward

DOUGLAS

R Wear

PERCY

NEVILLE

DURHAM

Ravine

ROKEBY

Cross +

Castle

Cathedral

R Browney

N

R Wear

☐ Scots

■ English

0   1 mile

Sunderland Bridge

↓ York

27

The Bender Stone, a standing stone which is supposed to mark the site of the battle (*Kevin Danforth/Northumberland Archaeological Group*)

The Bender Stone, a standing stone which is supposed to mark the site of the battle (*Kevin Danforth/Northumberland Archaeological Group*)

An early fourteenth-century sword (*Glasgow Art Gallery and Museum*)

After Halidon Hill there was a long period of peace in the Scottish borders, but in 1402 Sir Patrick Hepburn, Younger of Hailes, with a party of Scottish horsemen raided Northumberland. There was no political motive—it was probably only a sheep-stealing expedition. However on their return they were met by Lord Percy, Earl of Northumberland and the Earl of March, whose son, the Master of Dunbar, brought 200 men from the Berwick garrison to the fight at Nisbet Moor in Berwickshire, where the Scots were defeated and the popular young leader Hepburn killed.

When King Henry IV took an army to Wales to deal with Glendower's rising, the Scots collected an army commanded by the Earl of Douglas and Murdoch Stewart, son of the Duke of Albany, Governor of Scotland at the time, and crossed the border. Their army of 10,000 included, as had the army of David at the Standard, some lightly clad armed men from Galway under their leader Macdowall and these men must have struck terror in the English homes as they raided property as far south as Newcastle.

The English were not unprepared but, mindful of Nisbet, Percy, March and Hotspur decided to attack the Scots on their return journey. Collecting an army together at Dunstanburgh Castle, they set out for Wooler, camping on the River Till in a position that would block the passage of the Scots when they returned to Coldstream.

The Battle

Douglas with his booty-laden army reached Wooler before he realised the English were blocking his route north. He

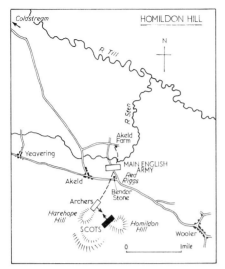

all the way to the Tweed, where, as in so many battles, 500 men were drowned.

Homildon Hill Today

The hill marked on the map as Humbleton Hill is Homildon Hill. The English archers were on Harehope Hill opposite. Red Riggs is on the other side of the A697; and a large stone known as the Bender Stone, with no inscription, near Akeld Farm is the only memorial. There is another stone at Yeavering but as bones have been dug up at Red Riggs it is assumed that this is where the main action took place.

The foot of Humbleton Hill showing the lower spur where the Scots were drawn up and the slope of Harehope running out of the picture on the right where Percy settled (*Kevin Danforth/Northumberland Archaeological Group*)

drew up his men on the flat-topped Homildon Hill. Here he waited for the English to attack. It was a good position and had he remained there he might have succeeded in winning the day, but on the hill opposite Percy's archers were drawn up, safe from direct assault because of the steep gorge in between. Having persuaded Hotspur's horsemen to wait at the bottom of the hill in a field known as Red Riggs, March directed the archers in their attack. They fired into the dense Scottish ranks and did dreadful execution. The semi-naked Galwegians suffered worst as they had no protection from the arrows at all.

The Scots could not get at the archers, but they were superior in numbers and Sir John Swinton, a border knight, determined to charge the main body at the foot of the hill. Accompanied by his old enemy Adam Gordon and about 100 horsemen armed with lances, they charged into the English ranks. The archers let them pass and Hotspur's men cut them to pieces. Douglas did not follow up the charge with his body of men until it was too late. Before they reached Red Riggs their numbers had been cut down by the terrible longbow. The English cavalry at last came into its own. Douglas was wounded in the eye and captured along with Stewart and the Earls of Angus and Moray. The retreating Scots were harried

Blore Heath/23 September 1459

The Wars of the Roses were a long-drawn-out struggle for the English Crown between the houses of York and Lancaster. The first action, at St Albans in 1455, was a Yorkist success. The Duke of Somerset and other leaders were killed but it was a small affair compared with the battles to come. The long passage of time between St Albans and Blore Heath, the second battle, was a period of uneasy truce. The Queen monopolised the King's Council with her Lancastrian favourites and in 1459, first secretly and then openly, distributed the badge of the swan (her son The Prince of Wales's emblem) to those who joined her forces. In September 1459 the Queen was at Eccleshall in Stafford-

however found that his route was blocked at Market Drayton and halted his army short of that town on Blore Heath, carefully concealing his two wings behind a slope and placing his centre beside the Hemphill Brook when he became aware of Audley's advance. There was time to dig a trench and put in sharp stakes and to draw up his waggons and carts on the flanks as a wall, Western style, against the renowned Cheshire archers.

The Battle

The first charge of Audley's horse—many of his knights were fighting on foot because of the muddy terrain—was beaten back and Salisbury withdrew his centre. The second charge enabled Audley to get across the brook, which is narrow but has very steep sides and must have proved an obstacle for any army with no portable bridges. The Yorkist archers took their toll and 500 of the Lancastrian bowmen changed sides unexpectedly, thus adding to Audley's discomfort. He was cut down and so were many other Lancastrian

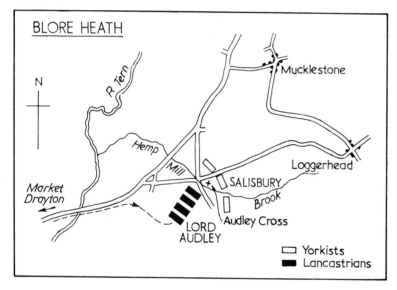

shire gathering troops; Lord Audley, with a party of Cheshire adherents to the Royalist or Lancastrian cause, was at Market Drayton. The Yorkists had retired to Ludlow and Lord Salisbury, with a force of about 3,000, was on the march from the Yorkist stronghold of Middleham, home of Richard of Gloucester, to Ludlow. The Yorkist plan was to unite the two armies and march on London. Queen Margaret's spies soon discovered it and the Queen ordered Lord Audley to intercept Salisbury (Father of the Earl of Warwick) and destroy him. Salisbury

Audley Cross (*author*)

leaders. Some 2,400 were killed by Salisbury's men, who were mostly armed with spears and bills. The Yorkist cannon, too, played their part. The surviving Lancastrians retreated to Eccleshall along the brook and at night Salisbury took his weary army onwards to Ludlow.

Aftermath

Although a resounding victory, the Yorkist cannon was captured by Margaret's army the next day. They had been left in charge of a friar who fired them from time to time, thus convincing the Queen that the Yorkists had camped on the heath during the night. At Ludford Bridge, outside Ludlow, the Lancastrians caught up with Salisbury and York and greatly outnumbered them. Talbot's Calais garrison, who had been pressed in to support York, defected to the King and although no battle was fought, the Yorkist forces dispersed and fled, so the advantage of Blore Heath was short-lived. As a single battle, though, it is a fine example of strategy outgunning larger numbers.

The Battlefield Today

Blore Heath is not easy to find. The cross is hidden in a large field to the left of the Newcastle-under-Lyme to Market Drayton road (A53) and is in a delapidated state. Its inscription used to read: 'On this spot was fought the Battle of Blore Heath in 1459; Lord Audley who commanded for the side of Lancaster was defeated and slain. To perpetuate the memory of the action & the place this ancient monument was repaired in 1765 at the charge of the Lord of the Manor, Charles Boothby Schrymsher.' Perhaps it will be repaired before it vanishes. In the village of Mucklestone is an anvil where the Queen is supposed to have had her horse's shoes taken off and reversed so that she escaped the battle without pursuit. This is very unlikely as she would have been behind the Yorkist lines and it is much more probable that she commanded the army that took over the cannon on the following day.

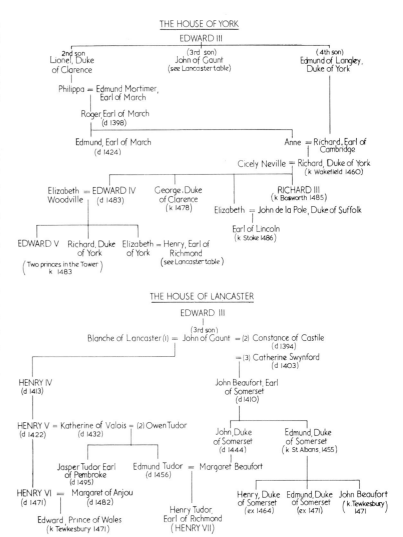

THE HOUSE OF YORK

EDWARD III

- 2nd son: Lionel, Duke of Clarence
- (3rd son) John of Gaunt (see Lancaster table)
- (4th son) Edmund of Langley, Duke of York

Philippa = Edmund Mortimer, Earl of March

Roger, Earl of March (d 1398)

Edmund, Earl of March (d 1424)

Anne = Richard, Earl of Cambridge

Cicely Neville = Richard, Duke of York (k Wakefield 1460)

Elizabeth Woodville = EDWARD IV (d 1483)

George, Duke of Clarence (k 1478)

RICHARD III (k Bosworth 1485)

Elizabeth = John de la Pole, Duke of Suffolk

Earl of Lincoln (k Stoke 1486)

EDWARD V   Richard, Duke of York   Elizabeth of York = Henry, Earl of Richmond (see Lancaster table)

(Two princes in the Tower k 1483)

THE HOUSE OF LANCASTER

EDWARD III

(3rd son)

Blanche of Lancaster (1) = John of Gaunt = (2) Constance of Castile (d 1394)

= (3) Catherine Swynford (d 1403)

HENRY IV (d 1413)

John Beaufort, Earl of Somerset (d 1410)

HENRY V = Katherine of Valois = (2) Owen Tudor (d 1422)   (d 1432)

John, Duke of Somerset (d 1444)

Edmund, Duke of Somerset (k St Albans 1455)

Jasper Tudor Earl of Pembroke (d 1495)

Edmund Tudor (d 1456) = Margaret Beaufort

HENRY VI (d 1471) = Margaret of Anjou (d 1482)

Henry, Duke of Somerset (ex 1464)

Edmund, Duke of Somerset (ex 1471)

John Beaufort (k Tewkesbury 1471)

Edward, Prince of Wales (k Tewkesbury 1471)

Henry Tudor, Earl of Richmond (HENRY VII)

The anvil on which Queen Margaret is supposed to have had her horseshoes reversed (*author*)

Northampton/10 July 1460

Northampton was the scene of a battle in the Baron's War, 1264–5, when Prince Edward defeated young Simon de Montfort; it has been called Henry III's only victory as the King took a major part in the action. However it involved the capture of the town, then walled with an important castle, rather than a pitched battle. In 1460 there was a larger, more important battle outside the town but strangely a defensive battle for the Lancastrians, rather like the second St Albans battle in reverse. After Blore Heath and the Ludford Bridge surprise, York himself went to Ireland and the Lancastrians captured London. Their leader, Lord Scales, father of Elizabeth Woodville, held the Tower and continued to hold it when the Yorkists landed at Sandwich and entered London.

The Queen with King Henry, who was a passenger in all the Wars of the Roses campaigns and left military matters to his capable wife, and other Lancastrians gathered an army at Coventry and headed south. The Duke of Buckingham had landed near Northampton and it may have been his suggestion to camp there. It was a strange decision because his camp was south of the river and although he entrenched it with a bank and sharp stakes, there was no obvious means of retreat as the River Nene was not fordable, at least not—as in July 1460—after heavy rain. The Lancastrian cannon guarded the road from London and the attempted intervention of the Archbishop of Canterbury and the Papal Legate could not prevent the forthcoming action. The Yorkists with Lord Falconburg in charge of the rear, Edward commanding the van

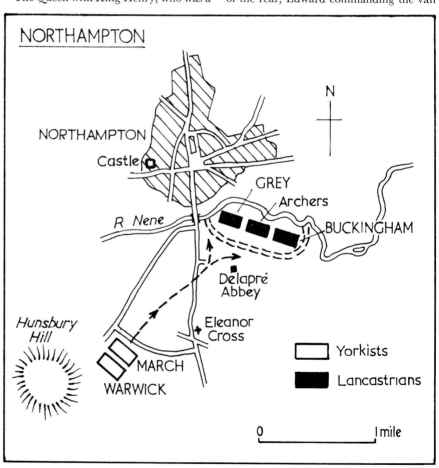

and Warwick the main body, camped on Hunsbury Hill, where traces of a hill-fort can still be seen. The Yorkists knew that they had to capture the King to bring any sort of peace to the land. They still sent the Bishop of Salisbury to Buckingham to ask him to surrender, for early on in the Wars of the Roses, battles were fought rather as a last resort.

The Battle

Before light the Yorkists attacked, Edward leading the way over the Nene marshes. Warwick's men had been ordered not to kill the men wearing the badge of the 'black ragged staff'. These were the Lancastrian right under Edmund, Lord Grey of Ruthin. Grey had plotted with Edward before the battle and agreed to take no part in the action if Edward supported his claim for Lord Fanhope's land at Ampthill. There were probably other reasons for Grey's treachery; in 1463 he became Lord Treasurer of England, and the bribe of a high office might have been the real carrot. Buckingham's cannon refused to work because of the

Delapré Abbey where King Henry VI spent the night after the battle (*author*)

rain, and although his archers in the centre found Edward's heavily armoured men easy to shoot down, the 'black ragged staff' men were helped by Warwick's force over the stockade and the battle was soon over, many Lancastrians being drowned attempting to get over the Nene. Lords Buckingham, Shrewsbury, Egremont and Beaumont were among the 300 slain and many were buried at nearby Delapré Abbey. The Queen and a few others escaped to Chester, and Henry IV was led captive to London, where Scales surrendered the Tower. York came over from Ireland and became Protector and heir apparent during Henry's lifetime.

The Battlefield Today

Very little can be seen of the battlefield. Delapré Abbey—now mostly a sixteenth- and nineteenth-century building—still stands off the A508 south of the city. It is open to the public on Saturday and Thursday afternoons and contains the County Record Office. The river site can be seen from Nunn Mills Road but it is mostly occupied by the Avon cosmetics firm. The old Eleanor Cross on the road to Buckingham where the Archbishop and the Legate stood to see the White Rose army go into action is still intact.

Eleanor Cross (*author*)

33

Wakefield/31 December 1460

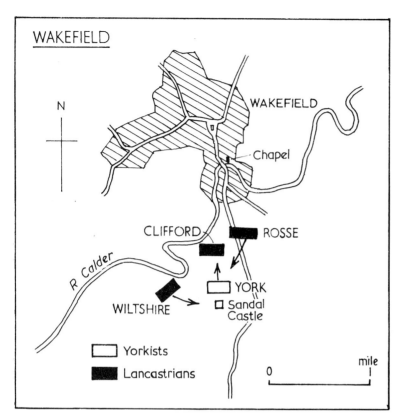

WAKEFIELD

N

WAKEFIELD

Chapel

CLIFFORD · ROSSE

R Calder

WILTSHIRE

YORK

☐ Sandal Castle

☐ Yorkists

■ Lancastrians

0   mile

When the Duke of York claimed the throne for himself after his success at Northampton, many thought he was claiming it illegally as Queen Margaret's son was the rightful heir to the throne. The Lancastrians were in Hull, but the Yorkists were divided, the Earl of March was on the Welsh border raising reinforcements and Warwick was in London, but Richard of York with the aged Earl of Salisbury and about 5,000 men set off from London and on Christmas Eve arrived at Sandal Castle, Wakefield. The Queen's army commanded by Lord Clifford, Lord Roos of Hamlake, and the Earl of Wiltshire was three times the size of York's, but as long as the latter held out at Sandal until the arrival of Edmund with his new army, he was safe.

The Battle

What induced the Duke to leave the safety of his castle and fight? It could

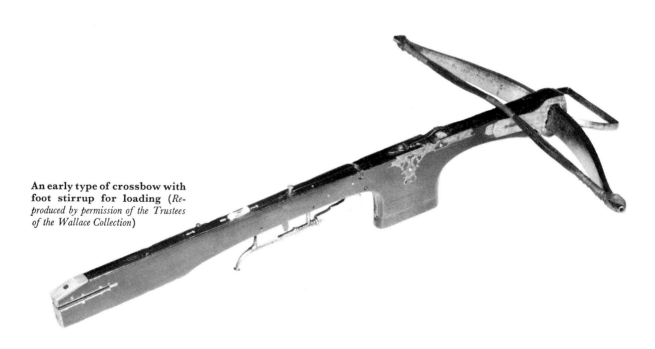

An early type of crossbow with foot stirrup for loading (*Reproduced by permission of the Trustees of the Wallace Collection*)

34

have been that he was short of food, but it was more likely due to the Queen's ruse. She placed Somerset's vanguard in full view of the castle, while she instructed the right wing under Wiltshire to remain hidden and the horse under Lord Roos to remain—roughly where the Victorian monument now stands—on the left also out of sight from the castle. Once York and Salisbury had left the castle and approached Somerset, the Queen and Clifford—nominally in command—sent Wiltshire in to capture the castle and Roos's horse to prevent York from retreating. The latter was 'caught like a fish unto a net' and hopelessly outnumbered. It is alleged that 2,800 Yorkists were killed including the Duke and his son Edmund, Earl of Rutland, who was caught by Clifford crossing the bridge and brutally murdered. The old Earl of Salisbury was beheaded at Pontefract the following day and the heads of the Yorkist leaders were impaled on the Micklegate Bar in York 'so York might overlook York'. Lord Clifford had his revenge for the death of his father at St Albans in 1455, but there were still two Yorkist leaders left, Edward of March and young Richard of Gloucester.

The Battlefield Today

The remains of Sandal Castle, recently excavated, can be seen at the end of Pinfold Grove off the A61. There is a chapel on the bridge at Wakefield reputably endowed by Edward IV in memory of his young brother, Edmund. Most of it dates from 1847; it is well preserved and used once a month. The façade of the old chapel is now a boathouse at Kettlethorpe Hall. A monument to the Duke of York was destroyed during the Civil War but a Victorian monument stands in the grounds of Manygates School with a carving of the Duke based on one that used to stand on the Welsh bridge at Shrewsbury. According to Scatcherd, author of *The Chapel of King Edward III*, the Bridge Chapel was built in 1357, so there is some doubt as to its connection with the murdered prince, who is more likely to have been murdered on the field of battle.

South view of Sandal Castle and the town of Wakefield (*National Monuments Record*)

Mortimer's Cross/2 February 1461

Croft Castle (*author*)

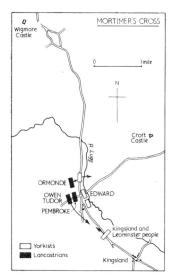

The Battle of Wakefield really marks the turning point in violence during the Wars of the Roses. Before then men were content to patch up quarrels; afterwards there were no holds barred. Young Edward, Earl of March, lost both his father and brother at Wakefield and must have been numbed by the news. He was in Gloucester when he heard that Jasper Tudor, Lord Pembroke and a party of French and Irish under the Earl of Wiltshire were in Wales and making for the Midlands. London was in Warwick's hands but Edward was determined to place his small army between London and the threat from Wales.

On the advice of his ally, Sir Richard Croft of Croft Castle, Edward positioned his troops in Wig Marsh, blocking the road the Lancastrians would be taking to Worcester. Behind him was the River Lugg, fordable in a few places but the only bridge was in the centre of the Yorkist position. Why didn't Edward place his army behind the river and beat the Lancastrian divisions one by one as they came over the bridge? Such a policy worked well at Stirling Bridge. Possibly because the river was fordable and the marsh was a better protection; more probably because he wanted to control the crossroads and

prevent the Lancastrians swinging to their right. What seems evident is that Edward's army was about 5,000 strong but his opponents were fewer—nearer 4,000 and untried in battle. Edward had a powerful contingent of archers which he placed in positions to guard the fords and bridge, as well as having many loyal supporters at Kingsland, who determined to keep out the Lancastrians.

The Battle

The battle had not commenced when Edward's men saw the strange sight of three suns in the sky. This parhelion was so unusual that the Yorkists took it for an omen of success and Edward had 'the sun in splendour' as his badge. The Lancastrian advance was as expected. Edward blocked Pembroke at the bridge where a heavy, slogging battle commenced. Butler, the Earl of Ormond, and Wiltshire, who was a capable commander, took his left wing through the ford to the left of the bridge and pushed back Edward's right flank. Owen Tudor in the rear made off to the right towards Kingsland, attempting to find an easier passage across the river. He was surrounded and captured by the men of Kingsland, supported by Edward's

36

left wing. The Yorkist archers took great toll of the mounted Lancastrians. A silver spur in Hereford Museum was found near the battlefield in 1839 and would appear to have come from a Lancastrian knight attempting to flee the battle. Two succeeded—Wiltshire and Pembroke—and the latter survived to come over with Richmond at Bosworth, but Owen Tudor, Sir John Scudamore and his two sons, and some others were executed in Hereford the following day. This action might have been in revenge for the slaughter after Wakefield, but the fact that Tudor had married the widow of Henry V made him a claimant to the throne and his grandson Henry Richmond was thus given more incentive to invade Wales in 1485. In the long run then, and not only for succession reasons, Mortimer's Cross was probably a Yorkist disaster, for Edward was prevented from coming to Warwick's aid at the second battle of St Albans.

The Battlefield Today

Mortimer's Cross has a large monument at the inn on the junction of the A4110 from Hereford and the B4360 from Leominster. There is only a crossroads garage and a hotel by the Lugg bridge. It is worth visiting nearby Croft Castle (owned by The National Trust), where Sir Richard Croft's tomb is in the church. He fought at Stoke and Tewkesbury as well as Mortimer's Cross. Wigmore Castle ruins are also worth a visit; Edward's grandmother, Anne Mortimer, lived here but it became a ruin at an early date.

The monument, now difficult to read, has the following inscription:

This pedestal is erected to perpetuate the memory of an obstinate bloody and decisive battle, fought near this spot, in the Civil Wars between the ambitious houses of York and Lancaster, on the 2nd day of February 1460 between the forces of Edward Mortimer Earl of March (afterwards Edward IV) on the side of York and those of Henry the Sixth on the side of

Mortimer's Cross monument (*author*)

Lancaster. The King's troops were commanded by Jasper Earl of Pembroke; Edward commanded his own in person and was victorious: the slaughter was great on both sides four thousand being left dead on the field, and many Welsh persons of the first distinction were taken prisoners, among whom was Owen Tudor (great-grandfather to Henry VIII and a descendant of the illustrious Cadwallader) who was afterwards beheaded at Hereford: this was the decisive battle which fixed Edward IV on the throne of England, who was proclaimed King in London on the fifthof March following. Erected by subscription in the year 1799.

St Albans (second battle)/16 February 1461

Typical armour and weapons including a pavise—a large shield stuck in the ground to protect the whole body

Queen Margaret moved south after her victory at Wakefield, ravaging the country and allowing her many Scottish troops freedom to pillage. Her slow progress permitted Warwick to move north and wait for her at St Albans, where he divided his army into three groups. One group, the weakest though it had most of his archers, remained in the town while the other two were positioned on the Harpenden and Sandridge roads. The use of caltraps and nets with spikes were recorded for keeping cavalry off the roads and Warwick's Burgundians had flaming arrows, primitive handguns firing darts and some crossbowmen with pavises. The two main groups could easily communicate via Beech Bottom, a sunken lane.

Margaret's army brushed aside a Yorkist detachment at Dunstable, where 200 Yorkists were killed and their leader, a local butcher, killed himself in shame. Warwick must have realised by now from his scouts that the Queen would not be advancing by the Harpenden road, yet he did not move the King from St Albans Abbey or strengthen his force in the town.

The Battle

During the early hours of 16 February the Lancastrians attacked up George Street and were driven back by Yorkist archers. They then attacked up Catherine Street, coming round to the back of the archers and, after a long struggle—the reverse of the First Battle of St Albans—the Yorkists were defeated.

Warwick now had to turn his army round and re-arrange his elaborate defences. Most of his caltraps were useless, being behind his lines. His cannon did very little damage and his handguns were more dangerous to their firers than to the enemy. It snowed and at a critical moment in the action a large Kentish division under Lovelace went over to the Queen's side. His left wing fled in disarray and he withdrew his men into a tight defensive position between Sandridge and Cheapside farm —the old Belgae line—until nightfall when he withdrew to Chipping Norton with

38

4,000 men. The Lancastrians were triumphant.

Results

The St Albans battle was one of the most decisive victories of the Wars of the Roses for the Lancastrians. It was to Warwick's credit that he managed to extricate so many of his troops and join up with the victorious army of Prince Edward of York, who was on his way from Mortimer's Cross, at Chipping Norton in the Cotswolds, and thus to proceed to the battlefield of Towton. Margaret rescued King Henry from the Abbey, who knighted young Prince Edward (of Wales), aged seven, on the field of battle. The boy was allowed by his mother to decide on the fate of some of the prisoners and it is said that his decisions—as to whether they should die by sword or axe—were as bloodthirsty as any of his elders. His end at Tewkesbury was to be similarly violent.

St Albans Today

The main area of the battle outside the town was at Bernard's Heath, now covered in houses. There is a public playground on the Sandridge Road near the Cricketer's Inn where the Yorkist left turned and fled. Warwick's final position was near the Old Albanians rugby ground. The Red Lion and the Fleur de Lys in the town must have been two of the buildings occupied by the Yorkist archers.

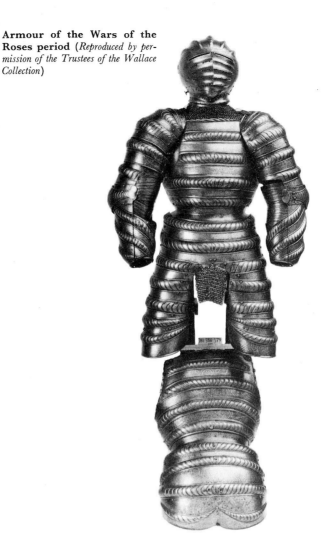

Armour of the Wars of the Roses period (*Reproduced by permission of the Trustees of the Wallace Collection*)

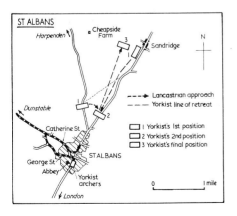

Towton/29 March 1461

The Lancastrian victories at Wakefield and St Albans might have convinced them that the Yorkists were almost defeated. However a Lancastrian army had been thoroughly beaten at Mortimer's Cross by young Prince Edward and Queen Margaret must have judged it was inadvisable to make for London when Edward's army remained undefeated. Edward instead entered the city in triumph and held a review of his troops in Clerkenwell fields on 2 March. The Earl of Warwick, Duke of Norfolk and Lord Falconberg, uncle of Warwick, were present and all were to play leading parts in the forthcoming battle. The Yorkists were angry at Queen Margaret's execution of prisoners after St

Albans, especially Lord Bonvile and Sir Thomas Kiriel who had been looking after Henry VI and took no part in the fighting. On 7 March the Yorkists marched north for Pontefract collecting support there; meanwhile the Lancastrians were at York in some strength—30,000 according to Hall's chronicle but it is unlikely if they were in such numbers or that Edward's army was as large as 25,000.

There were two preliminary skirmishes. Firstly Lord Fitzwalter, who was sent ahead by Edward with some troops to capture the crossing over the River Aire at Ferrybridge, was cut down by Lord Clifford and his Lancastrian horse. Few escaped and Yorkist morale dropped so low that Warwick killed his horse and determined to fight on foot. Crossing the river at Castleford instead, Edward's vanguard under Lord Fauconberg and his men from Kent caught Clifford's horse in Dintingdale and a lucky arrow killed Clifford. On the eve of Palm Sunday the two armies drew up facing each other, the Lancastrians on Towton ridge with the River Cock on their right wing, the Yorkists on a smaller ridge with the Cock on their left and the village of Saxton behind them.

The Battle

Palm Sunday dawned with driving snow. The Yorkist archers took advantage of the wind which was in their favour and firing into it they then stepped back. The Lancastrians misjudged the wind and the distance and fired short, allowing the Yorkist archers to pick up the arrows and re-use them. Northumberland and Somerset in the Lancastrian van pressed forward and many lightly armed Yorkist archers were killed. Warwick held on grimly and on his left Edward's men gave way in Castle Hill Wood. For two hours the slogging match went on and neither side gave ground until the outnumbered Yorkists were suddenly relieved by the late arrival of the Duke of Norfolk's forces. The Duke was ill (he died later in the year and it was his son who fought at Bosworth) but his men arrived and were sent forward to outflank the Lancastrian left wing. The sudden arrival of fresh troops was too much for the hard-pressed Lancastrians and they started giving way. Many were drowned in the Cock and others pressed on to Tadcaster, where they found the bridge had been destroyed. They were either hewn down by Wenlock's men who pursued them into the town or else drowned in the River Wharfe. There was no quarter given on Edward's orders; Lord Dacre, resting in a field called North Acre, took off his helmet for a drink from a stream and was shot by a boy hiding in an elder tree. The Queen and her son

escaped to Scotland. The luckless King Henry was captured.

After the battle the Earls of Wiltshire and Devon were beheaded and most of the dead of both sides were flung into two large pits. The chroniclers give the dead as 28,000 but a more reliable figure is 9,000. Brooke mentions that before he visited the battlefield in 1857 the owner of Towton Hall had enlarged his cellars and a great quantity of bones had been found.

The Battlefield Today

Towton is easily found: leave York by the A64 and turn onto the A162 at Tadcaster. The first hamlet you come to is Towton and Lord Dacre's cross is beside the road (B1217) that leads from Towton to Saxton. The Bloody Meadow is to the right in the curve of the Cock. Here too is Castle Hill Wood where Edward's men had difficulty containing Northumberland. It can be reached by a footpath to Low Leads where the remains of burial mounds can still be seen. Lord Dacre's tomb stands in Saxton churchyard.

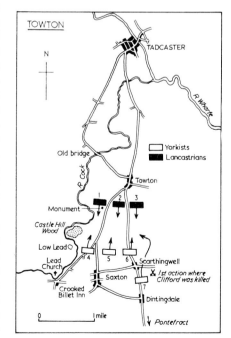

1 Northumberland
2 Somerset
3 Exeter
4 Edward
5 Falconberg
6 Warwick
7 Norfolk's men (Norfolk himself was absent)

41

Barnet/14 April 1471

An early engraving of the 1740 monument

Towton placed the Yorkists in power. Edward IV was placed on the throne but the Lancastrian cause was by no means dead. Edward made himself unpopular by marrying Elizabeth Woodville, and the Woodvilles were arch enemies of Warwick, who plotted with Queen Margaret to put Henry back on the throne. Edward was forced to flee to Burgundy from Kings Lynn and Henry was replaced on the throne. Warwick ruled; his brother Montagu had an army at Pontefract, Oxford was watching the east coast and the Earl of Pembroke was in Wales. With Falconberg commanding the fleet the position was dim for Edward.

Edward was an optimist however. He landed at Ravenspur with about 2,000 men and proceeded south, where he was joined by Sir William Stanley, Sir James Harrington and others until by the time he approached Coventry, where Warwick was waiting for both Montagu and Clarence, a battle seemed imminent. Instead, Clarence welcomed Edward with open arms and joined him with his force so that the two brothers entered London in triumph. The Tower was captured, Yorkist prisoners released and, with reinforcements, Edward could now turn

in his tracks and deal with Warwick who had positioned his army at Barnet. Time was on Warwick's side as he was expecting the Queen to send help. Placing Oxford's forces on his right wing, Montagu in the centre and Exeter on the left, Warwick commanded the reserve in the place where the present monument stands.

Edward arrived in the dark. On his left was Hastings, who had crossed with him from Burgundy, on his right the young Richard of Gloucester. Edward himself commanded the centre with the unfortunate Henry, a prisoner, in the reserve.

The Battle

There are aspects of Barnet that are similar to Marston Moor but in general it was a battle of division-*v*-division with little co-operation or overall leadership on either side. The fog everywhere on 14 April confused both armies. Warwick fired his guns throughout the night to little effect. Oxford's men wore the badge of the radiant star, not too dissimilar to Edward's badge of the sun with rays that he had adopted since his victory at Mortimer's Cross (*see* p 36). He charged first on Hasting's division, cutting it to pieces and pursuing it for some miles.

Richard made some progress against Exeter but, finding he was outflanked, Exeter moved round to link up with Warwick facing east where Richard's attack was coming from. In the centre Montagu wheeled round too, possibly to keep in touch with Exeter and possibly because Edward was also changing his position to keep up with Gloucester.

The returning Earl of Oxford was greeted by Montagu with a shower of arrows, his archers confusing the sign of the star with Edward's sign of the sun. Their approach from the south must also have spread confusion. There were cries of 'Treason, Treason' and Montagu was killed, possibly by one of Oxford's men in retaliation.

Warwick withdrew to a wood, where he had left his horse. Here he was overtaken by less heavily armed men and killed. Of the Lancastrian leaders, only Oxford and Exeter, who was badly wounded, escaped. Margaret landed at Weymouth too late to save the Lancastrian cause.

Barnet Today

Take the A1 from London to the junction with the A411 to Barnet, now a commuter suburb. Turning down the high street to Hadley Green, the monument erected in 1740 stands at a road junction. On the left is the golf course, where Oxford must have started his attack on Hastings, and on the right Hadley Common where Richard held his ground. The best viewpoint, with permission from the golfers, is probably obtained from the third tee on the golf course.

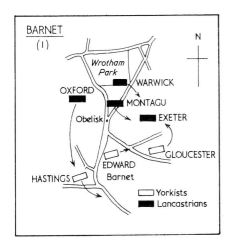

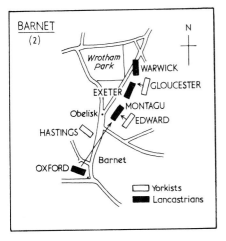

The death of the Earl of Warwick (*Radio Times Hulton Picture Library*)

Tewkesbury/14 May 1471

Gupshill Manor built in 1430, where Queen Margaret spent the night before the battle (*author*)

With some French soldiers, Prince Edward and his mother Queen Margaret landed at Weymouth on the day of the Battle of Barnet. In spite of the grim news, Margaret's supporters promised to help and the Earl of Pembroke set off for Wales and others went north to get support. King Edward had disbanded his army after Barnet before he heard of the Queen's arrival and he promptly set about raising a new force. He established his headquarters at Windsor Castle and, with Lord Hastings and Richard of Gloucester as his two commanders, he was soon on his way to attempt to block Margaret's route to Wales.

The Queen arrived at Bristol on 1 May and gained some support, though mainly in arms and artillery rather than men. Meanwhile Edward was in Malmesbury. Sending her van to Sodbury Hill the Queen pushed on to Gloucester via Berkeley Castle, where she spent the night. Her vanguard at Sodbury captured some of Edward's quartermasters and Edward, confused, spent the night on Sodbury Hill, not realising until morning that his opponents had given him the slip. He at once sent messengers to Sir Richard Beauchamp, Governor of Gloucester, to close his gates to Margaret. The messengers must have taken a different route to Margaret, for when she arrived at the town early in the morning the gates were already closed. Maybe Beauchamp was a Yorkist and had anticipated Edward's message. The weary Lancastrian army had no choice but to push north to Tewkesbury where they could cross into Wales. Beauchamp captured some of their Bristol guns before they got away. When Margaret finally reached Tewkesbury her exhausted men were too tired to cross the river and she camped in a motte and bailey castle, still visible, at Gupshill. Edward, whose army was also exhausted, stopped at Tredington, a few miles out of the town on the Cheltenham road. His army had come over Birdlip hill via Prinknash Abbey; although less in number than the Lancastrians—about 3,500 to their 5,000—in morale and arms they were superior.

The Battle

Margaret's army, nominally commanded by the Duke of Somerset, was positioned facing south at Gupshill, with Wenlock, a

Queen Margaret made a prisoner of Edward IV after the battle (*Radio Times Hulton Picture Library*)

former Yorkist, in the centre, Devonshire on the left wing and Somerset himself on the right. With Wenlock was the young Prince Edward, aged 17 and eager to gain his spurs. King Edward's army came across the Swillgate Brook and near Stonehouse Farm changed line to column, rather like the Jacobites before Prestonpans (*see* p 112). On the left was Richard of Gloucester, the King held the centre and Lord Hastings the right. The Swillgate was on one flank but on Richard's flank there was a park and, being May, the trees concealed 200 spearmen positioned by Edward to stop any flanking moves by Somerset. The latter had indeed made an early flanking move intending to get behind Richard's men. Somerset had planned that Wenlock should make a simultaneous frontal attack on Gloucester's position, which was a mass of 'evil land and deep dykes'. Thus when Somerset's men disappeared in The Park passing up behind a hillock they were set upon not only by part of Richard's force but by the small band of spearmen who noisily attacked their rear. Had Wenlock attacked the Lancastrians might have won the day, but he was disinclined to leave his position. He left Somerset to his own devices and the latter, returning with the loss of many men who fell in the Bloody Meadow, was so incensed that he accused his fellow commander of treachery and before the luckless Wenlock could reply, Somerset had dashed out his brains with his mace.

The Rout

The Lancastrian army now lost all hope of success and panic set in. There was a rush to get over the river: many were cut down by the Abbey mill, others like Somerset sought sanctuary in the Abbey itself. They were dragged out, tried in haste and executed in the market place. The young prince was killed and his mother escaped to Little Malvern, where she was later captured and imprisoned in the Tower for five years. The Yorkist victory was complete.

The Battlefield Today

Probably the best starting place is Gupshill Inn, which was rebuilt in the seventeenth century on the site of a building that must have been there in 1471. Opposite was Margaret's camp in the remains of the motte and bailey castle. The hillock is still visible in a field behind Gupshill near the A38. The area to the west of Stonehouse Farm is still called The Park. Bloody Meadow is marked by a

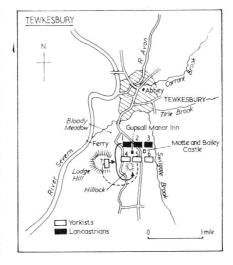

1 Somerset
2 Wenlock
3 Devonshire
4 Richard of Gloucester
5 King Edward IV
6 Hastings
7 Yorkist spearmen

signboard. In the town museum there is a model of the battle which is unreliable as, like Bosworth, only part of the two armies were in action. Lord Hastings did not take much part and neither did the King's right wing. In fact, in spite of the barbarity shown to the Lancastrian leaders, the rank and file were allowed to surrender their arms and go home. The Abbey has a door in the sacristy that was refaced with bits and pieces of armour captured from Lancastrians. The unfortunate Clarence—Richard's brother who was drowned in a butt of malmsey wine—and his wife were buried here and unsqueamish visitors can see his skull and a few bones behind a little glass window.

Bosworth Field/22 August 1485

One of the interpretative sign-boards erected at Bosworth Field (*By courtesy of the County Estates Surveyor's Department, Leicestershire County Council*)

The memorial stone in King Richard's Field, said to be where he was struck down (*By courtesy of the County Estates Surveyor's Department, Leicestershire County Council*)

The invasion force of Henry of Richmond set sail from France on 1 August 1485. With 2,000 French mercenaries and a few loyal supporters like the Earl of Oxford and the Earl of Pembroke, Henry Richmond's army must have been deeply concerned about their chance of success. Richmond was no soldier and was not sure about the support he would get, though he had sent word to the two Stanleys before his ships reached Milford Haven. Three hundred and twelve years later another invasion force from France landed on the same coast (*see* Fishguard p 120). It was too difficult for Richard, whose main strength was in the north and east, to get to grips with his adversary and he set up his headquarters at Nottingham. Thomas Howard, Earl of Norfolk, was his main supporter with his son, the Earl of Surrey. The Earl of Northumberland brought his northerners to Nottingham and Sir Robert Brackenbury, Governor of the Tower, brought his knights, some of whom like Walter Hungerford deserted to Richmond en route for Nottingham.

Richmond—without the Stanleys, who had allowed him free passage through their lands but refused to give him open support—commanded an army of 5,000. He had some French gunners with serpentines firing stone balls and a few Welsh archers.

Richard's army was twice this size. Norfolk's van alone was nearly 8,000 strong, mostly archers and billmen. Northumberland had 3,000 and the King had 1,000 mounted men. The Stanley's combined force of 4,500 would add a decisive blow on either side but which side would they join?

Camping on 21 August near Sutton Cheney, Richard held a night service in Sutton Cheney church; early in the morning his scouts rushed out to secure Ambion Hill. This narrow hill commands the area and, assuming there were then fewer trees, Richard would have had no problem in seeing Richmond's advance from White Moors and the two Stanley camps. The banners would have identified the forces. Norfolk lined the hill looking

west; Northumberland turned to look north—his army would not have had space to deploy in any other way other than south which was unnecessary; Richard kept in the centre with his picked knights waiting for a chance to join up with Sir William Stanley who, unlike his outlawed brother, was still expected to prove loyal.

The Battle

Most of the action took place on the slope before Glebe Farm. Richmond, with his right commanded by Talbot, his left by Sir John Savage—though he too expected Stanley to join him there—and his centre by Jasper, Earl of Pembroke, relied on his van under the redoubtable Earl of Oxford, whom we last saw causing havoc at Barnet due to his impetuous charge. Commanding his men not to move more than ten paces from his banners, which he planted in a semicircle, and arranging them in a tight wedge, Oxford prepared for Norfolk's charge. The stone balls from the cannon on either side do not seem to have done much damage, but the archers must have done. The Oxford–Norfolk battle went on for two hours, neither side giving way, and when Norfolk was killed his son Surrey took over.

King Richard was desperate—he was an impatient man at the best of times. Commanding Catesby to kill Lord Strange, he spotted Richmond's banners moving over towards Sir William Stanley and decided a charge would end the day. If he killed Richmond, then the Stanleys would have to support him. Sir William's horsemen were approaching and Richard must have timed his attack, more an ambush than a charge, to the second. With about eighty knights he rushed down on the little group round Richmond. His lance killed Sir William Brandon, Richmond's standard bearer, and he dashed Sir John Cheney to the ground with a blow from his battleaxe. Sir William Stanley's Cheshire horsemen now caught up with him and the King's horse was killed, then the King, fighting madly, died surrounded by the enemy. The battle was over. Someone found the crown in a thorn hedge and placed it on Richmond's head. Northumberland's men escaped to the north without ever having fought at all. Richard's body was taken to Leicester, stripped naked over a horse, accompanied by his standard carried by the White Boar Herald. There was a pursuit as far as Stoke Golding. Catesby was captured and later executed; Lord Strange was re-united with his father; Northumberland was pardoned. But the shifty Sir William Stanley was executed on a trumped-up charge of treason ten years later; even Richmond, who owed his crown to his conduct, could not trust him in the end.

The Battlefield Today

Just north of Atherstone, the best way to Ambion Farm is via the road to Sutton Cheney. Look in the church to see the heraldic kneelers and the brass plate to Richard, erected by the Richard III Society. Then proceed towards Ambion Farm, which was turned into a superbly designed tourist centre by the Leicestershire County Council and others in 1974. The footpath round the battlefield is worth taking and King Dick's Well should be seen. There is a restaurant, a filmshow, a model-diorama with commentary, a museum and a bookstall as well as a picnic spot. Nearby Shenton station is also an information centre and there is a nature trail. Richard's stone is best seen from here. The map of the battle is the only controversial element of the battlesite.

Improbabilities of the Bosworth Field Battleplan

My account of Bosworth does not follow entirely the account of the battle by Dr D. T. Williams of Leicester University, which has been accepted as the basis for the excellent plans and diorama at Ambion Farm. The King was probably killed 'at a place called Sandeford' where the modern stone stands near Shenton station, and not at the site of the Well.

It is unlikely that both Stanleys were so near each other and that some of Lord

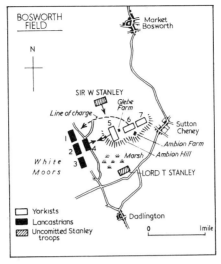

1	Savage
2	Jasper
3	Talbot
4	Oxford
5	Norfolk
6	Richard
7	Northumberland

Stanley's men charged with Sir William Stanley's horsemen. Lord Stanley was a declared outlaw and Richard held his son, Lord Strange, as a hostage on the top of Ambion Hill. Sir Thomas More's *History of King Richard III* first appeared in 1543 and gives Lord Thomas Stanley's army as 'being in the midst betwixt both hosts' and all accounts agree that the Stanley forces kept at least a mile apart. I think that Sir William Stanley spent the night before the battle at Near Cotton, but his brother was near Greenhill Farm between Dadlington and Shenton. This would mean that Lord Stanley would have had to cross the marsh to attack Richard's army, but he would not have known about the marsh and, like North-umberland who was able to argue that he was watching Sir William, he may not have been keen to fight at all.

The diorama is excellent; similar projects should be undertaken for more battles—Naseby for example is near enough to make an excellent joint trip.

Part of the exhibition at the Battlefield Centre (*By courtesy of the County Estates Surveyor's Department, Leicestershire County Council*)

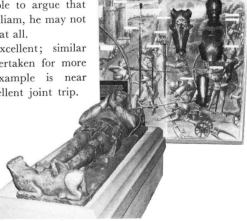

Stoke/16 June 1487

Bosworth Field was not the end of the Wars of the Roses. Two years later Lord Lovell, one of the survivors of Richard's army, and Robert de la Pole, Earl of Lincoln, assembled an army in Dublin. They had a trump card in the form of Lambert Simnel, a ten-year-old who they proclaimed to be one of the lost Princes of the Tower. He was proclaimed King Edward VI. Lincoln, who had a fairly strong claim to the throne himself (*see* p 31), as he was a nephew of Edward IV, was wealthy enough to employ a strong force of 2,000 German mercenaries under Schwartz. They landed in Lancashire in June and, with Irish and English contingents, the force numbered about 9,000. It was a formidable force. Crossing the Pennines, Lincoln halted at Masham and sent a messenger requesting permission to enter York. This was refused so he made for Southwell, perhaps thinking of getting to Newark. Crossing the River

Trent at Fiskerton ford, he waited for the Royal army to approach from Nottingham. There is some confusion over the accounts of the progress of the Royal army, but all accounts say King Henry was at Kenilworth when he heard of Lincoln's landing. Setting out via Coventry and Leicester he gathered troops en route. Reaching Nottingham on 14 June he was met by Lord Stanley now the Earl of Derby, and his son, Lord Strange, who had survived his time as Richard's hostage at Bosworth. The Royal Army was by now 12,000 men and commanding its vanguard was the veteran Earl of Oxford. No finer soldier fought for King Henry VII and another veteran, Lord Pembroke, who had escaped after Tewkesbury, was also present with the King. Carrying the Royal shield was Thomas Brandon, brother of the unfortunate standard bearer at Bosworth; yet another member of the Brandon family, Robert, was present, determined to seek vengeance for the luckless Sir William.

The Battle

Stoke was fought in two stages. The first stage went in favour of Lincoln, who had

48

positioned his Germans in the centre, his Irish, 'beggarly, naked and almost unarmed' on the left, while he held the right wing himself. Oxford's vanguard arrived before the main Royal army, which had perhaps dallied at Nottingham to collect latecomers. Lincoln's army descended the slope—it is not really a hill, though there were windmills there—to meet it. The Germans armed with crossbows fought hard and it was not until Henry's archers appeared that the tide of battle turned. Schwartz, Lincoln and Broughton were killed and many of the Irish took to their heels. The route to the ford, a narrow defile, became known as Red Gully because so many rebels perished there.

One leader escaped: Lord Lovell forced his horse into the water and rode across the ford. He was never seen again, but in 1708 some men repairing a chimney at his home, Minster Lovell in Oxfordshire, found a secret room with the skeleton of a man 'sitting at a table which was before him with a book, paper, pen etc; in another part of the room lay a cap'. The family considered this to be Lovell.

Lambert Simnel was captured and forced to work in the Royal kitchens. Robert Brandon was knighted on the field. Most of Oxford's first line were killed and it may have been Brandon who led the second line forward to reinforce him. The key moment in the battle was the death of Schwartz, for it was his contingent that held the rebel line together for three

Paul Dayrell and his wife who died in 1491, indicating the dress and armour of the Wars of the Roses period

hours; the Royal archers seem to have played, as so often happened, the principal part in Henry's victory.

Henry went to Lincoln to give thanks in the cathedral. He was almost free of the Yorkist claims. There was only one surviving male Yorkist claimant, the young Earl of Warwick. He was executed in 1499 and the Lancastrians were supreme. Bosworth and Stoke together were the really decisive victories of the Wars of the Roses. They may not have been as large as Towton or Barnet and by all accounts Henry VII was no soldier, but he seemed to be fortunate in his generals—Oxford the bold, Pembroke the lucky, and the Stanleys who were the main props to the Tudors in the North West.

The Battlefield Today

The village of Stoke is three miles south of Newark on the A46 and is known as East Stoke today. Fiskerton can be found by taking the turning past Stoke Hall to the river. The latter does not look fordable today. There is a small monument standing on private farmland near the river. Lincoln's monument can be seen at Wingfield Church, Suffolk. He lies with his wife, his hands raised in prayer; his armour even in stone appears well used.

A silver groat c1500 with the head of Henry VII (*Reproduced by courtesy of the Trustees of the British Museum*)

49

Flodden/9 September 1513

Close combat at Flodden

Henry VIII took his army to France in 1513 and King Louis XII called on Scotland, his ally, for help. King James IV, who was a man of honour though not a strategist, was quick to accept the offer to invade England. He collected a large army from all over Scotland and on 22 August 1513, crossed the Tweed at Coldstream. He had nearly 60,000 men including five huge cannon known as curtals firing 60lb shot, and seven small field-pieces—the Seven Sisters of Borthwick, for Robin Borthwick was James's Master Gunner—with small touch-holes and a long range, as well as other smaller guns. The French sent 6,000 18 feet Swiss pikes as well as a small force under d'Aussi, a French knight, to train James's army. The Scots were under their clan leaders and, as at Pinkie later, the only cavalry were the Earl of Home's borderers, but James's new tactics and the boggy ground decreed that these men fought on foot with Huntly's Highlanders, a strange combination. Lord Bothwell commanded the Scottish reserve, which included the Ettrick archers and many Lowland levies.

The Provost of Edinburgh brought his own contingent to the field.

The English commander was Henry's General of the North, Thomas Howard, Earl of Surrey, the seventy-year-old veteran of Richard III's defeated army at Bosworth. His army was small compared with the Scots—some 26,000—but better equipped. The Earl's elder son, Thomas Howard, Admiral of England, brought his ships' captains and their companies. They included Sir William Sidney of the *Great Barque*, Maurice Berkeley of the *Mary George*, James King of the *Julian of Dartmouth* and about 12 others with their ships' men, who were in those days mostly soldiers. The right wing was commanded by Surrey's younger son, Edmund Howard, and the border horse under Lord Dacre provided the only mounted arm. Most of Surrey's soldiers were armed with the billhook. Basically a siege weapon to aid climbing walls, it was effective against pikes, being much easier to wield. Dacre's men had lances. Unlike the Scots with their two-handed claymores, the English had shorter swords, more and better trained archers but were inferior in artillery. Most of Surrey's men were 'indentured retainers' including Lord Stanley's men, treated with suspicion by Surrey's men as they had fought for Henry Richmond at Bosworth against Surrey.

The Approach

The Scots were content with capturing Norham, Etal and Ford castles and then moved out to camp at Flodden Hill, described by an English observer as 'enclosed in three parts with three great mountains, so that there was no passage or entry but one way'. This way was the route from the north between the marshy River Till and the hill, and it was well covered by James's artillery.

Surrey's camp at Wooler was struck on 8 September and, guided by local men, the English army crossed the Till to the east bank and headed north to Doddington Moor. James was worried that the English might push on to Edinburgh and avoid him, but the English herald had already sent a message asking the Scots to descend and fight the following day; James was so unconcerned that he did not bother to guard the River Till crossings. Camping on Bar Moor the English were short of food and Surrey realised that he must fight the following day to save his army from starvation. Admiral Howard made the plans and set off early the next day with his vanguard to Twizel Bridge (the present bridge was probably built in the same style as the original one). The rearguard and main force under Surrey crossed the Till at Heaton Mill ford, both groups being undetected by the Scots. James was quick to call a conference when he spotted the English advance and he decided to move to Branxton Hill to prevent it being seized by the English. He ordered his artillery to be moved there, but this could not be done quickly as most of it was dug in.

Under the smoke of the fires of his camp, James set up his troops in four main groups and a reserve facing Piper's Hill and the village of Branxton. The English arrived in six divisions but Surrey hastily reformed them as five with Lord Dacre in reserve. The English artillery was soon in action but the Scots had left some of theirs behind protecting Ford Castle and when it did open fire it was mostly aimed too high; very early on a lucky English shot killed Borthwick, so the Scottish artillery took little part in the battle. Admiral Howard's vanguard, arriving first, could have been destroyed by James before Surrey and Stanley's men were in position but this was against the rules of chivalry and James was sure of his commanding position anyway.

The Battle

Flodden can best be described as a four-stage battle. Firstly, the Scots were horrified that their King wanted to become an infantryman; he decided to fight at the head of his picked knights and discarded his horse. Initially though he allowed Lord Home and Huntly's men to

Twizel Bridge (*author*)

51

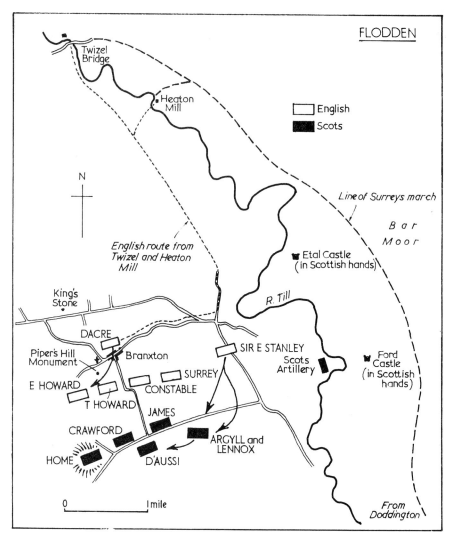

FLODDEN

Twizel Bridge

Heaton Mill

English
Scots

N

Line of Surreys march

Bar Moor

English route from Twizel and Heaton Mill

Etal Castle (in Scottish hands)

R. Till

King's Stone

DACRE

Piper's Hill Monument

Branxton

SIR E STANLEY

Scots Artillery

Ford Castle (in Scottish hands)

E HOWARD

SURREY

CONSTABLE

T HOWARD

JAMES

CRAWFORD

HOME

D'AUSSI

ARGYLL and LENNOX

0   1 mile

From Doddington

attack the English right wing under Sir Edmund Howard. The Scots' charge turned over the English banner and a portion of the Cheshire men fled in disarray but John Heron's Northumberland men stood firm and Lord Dacre came down from the reserve to put Huntly's Highlanders to flight. The Earl of Home's men made off to their horses taking many prisoners, but took little further part in the battle, watching on the hill to see which way things would turn out.

The second stage was the descent of the Scottish centre under the Earls of Montrose, Crawford and Errol as well as James

with levelled pikes and heavily armed men in front; there was little the English archers could do to stop them. 'Though the Scots fought sore and valiantly with their swords—for they shortly disappointed themselves of the long spears which were their greatest trust—yet they could not resist the bills that lighted so thick and sore about them.' For two hours the fighting went on.

The third stage was the action of Sir Edward Stanley. His left wing was late arriving and by the time it was in position the only Scottish contingent left on the hill was that of Argyle and Lennox.

Taking his men round by Marden farm, he pushed his archers forward to take the Scots, who were nominally commanded by the Frenchman d'Aussi, in the rear. There was a separate battle and the Scots were attacked on two sides at once. The Earls of Lennox, Argyle and Caithness were killed and two Scottish standards were captured singlehanded by Sir William Molyneux.

Lord Bothwell's men now joined their King and gradually the tide turned against Surrey's centre. However, Sir Edmund, now reinforced by Lord Dacre, attacked the

Conclusion

Flodden was the biggest Scottish defeat ever. Thousands were slain and one man alone of the Ettrick contingent of archers is supposed to have returned home. The 'Flowers of the Forest' pipe lament was composed in their honour. Henry VIII gave Surrey the Dukedom of Norfolk, the Admiral becoming Earl of Surrey instead and Sir Edward Stanley, who had done so much to win the battle, was created Lord Monteagle. Some 1,700 Englishmen died but the number of Scots slain was probably five times greater.

men of Crawford and Montrose in the rear and Stanley moved in from the other flank. James, fighting desperately, fell with thirty men, cut down by the English billhooks. His naked body was found the following day, recognised by Lord Dacre who knew him well. Some say his body was buried at St Michael's Church, Cornhill, in London after remaining unburied at Sheen Palace for several years; others in the Scottish camp said that the King escaped abroad and that the English found the wrong corpse, but his ring, dirk and sword were for many years with the College of Heralds in London.

Flodden Today

Best seen from the A697 from Morpeth to Coldstream, there is a small road to Branxton village and the monument stands clearly visible on the hill above the village. The tomb of Sir William Molyneux can be seen at Sefton, Lancashire, and an iron arrowhead, two metal cannonballs and three stone ones have been discovered on the site by a local man. Etal, Norham and Ford castles are well worth a visit.

The monument at Flodden
(*British Tourist Authority*)

Ancrum Moor/17 February 1545

Peniel Heugh with the monument on its summit (*author*)

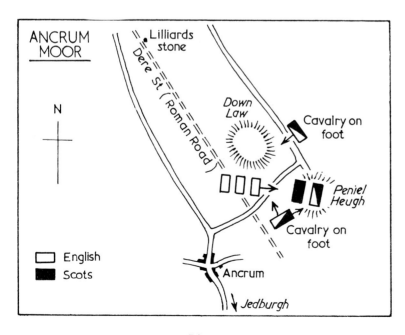

Towards the end of Henry VIII's reign affairs with Scotland took a turn for the worse. The Pope appointed Archbishop Beaton of St Andrews as one of his cardinals and the Scots rejected Henry's marriage plans for Edward to the infant Mary, Queen of Scots. At war with France, Henry could not do anything to encourage the 'auld alliance' between Scotland and France.

Henry determined to take his revenge on Scotland and sent the Earl of Hertford to Leith with a raiding party by sea. Hertford not only burnt Leith but also attacked Edinburgh where the Regent, Arran, was too weak to stop him. In the Borders two knights, Sir Brian Latour and Sir Ralph Evers, raided and burnt at will. With Henry's encouragement, Evers and Latour returned to England and raised an army of 5,000 to do further pillage in 1545. This army consisted of 1,500 Borderers, some of them from broken Scottish clans eager to obtain more land, and 3,000 were foreign mercenaries. The rest were the mob who had followed the two knights the year before. Entering Scotland via Jedburgh, they burnt Broomhouse Tower killing its lady and her family, and then pillaged Melrose Abbey and the tombs of the Douglas family. Archibald Douglas, Earl of Angus, whose lands were threatened by the English, joined with Norman Leslie, Master of Rothes, and Scott of Buccleuch to form a small Scottish army of scarcely half that number. The Scots horse were armed with lances and the foot with the Jedburgh staff, a wicked billhook on one side with an additional metal hook on the other for pulling riders off their horses. Advised by the cool Scott, Angus arranged his army on the low ground near Jedburgh between Lilliard's Edge and Peniel Heugh. The English, camped on Ancrum Moor, saw the Scots army appear to retreat. In fact the mounted men had given their horses to the camp followers and grooms and sent them to the top of a nearby hill, which to English eyes looked as if the Scots were retreating. It was a subtle plan.

The Battle

To climb from Ancrum Moor up Down Law and down the other side is exhausting and the fitter members of the English army arrived first, followed by the breathless mercenaries. All attempt at order was lost and they must have been astonished to see the neat ranks of the Scottish army arranged in three groups, horsemen fighting on foot on the wings and the billmen in the centre.

Bowes and Latour leading the English horse were in front and bore the brunt of the Scottish charge when it came. Horses reeled, the men with the Jedburgh staffs hooked down their riders, Latour included, and other Scots cut them to pieces as they lay on the ground. Meanwhile the mercenaries found that the smoke from their harquebusses was blown in their faces as both sun and wind were against the English. They wavered and and fell back, whereupon the 700 Borderers changed sides, so that the mercenaries, blinded by smoke, no longer knew friend from foe. With cries of 'Remember Broomhouse' the Scottish spearmen advanced and finished off the work of the billmen.

The Scots pursued their enemies off the hill. Watching Jedburgh townsfolk joined in the pursuit, women as well. One of these was maiden Lilliard, who gave her name to Lilliard's Edge near the battlefield. Her lover had been killed by Evers' men and she dashed in on his horse, continuing to fight although she lost both her legs. Her monument stands on the summit of the ridge, about a mile from the battlefield. Some think that she did not exist and that the monument was constructed to perpetuate this myth.

The result of this battle was the decision of Francis I to send an invading force to Portsmouth and French troops attacked the Isle of Wight. Angus regained his self-respect, for he had been suspected of being in Henry's pay, and Scotland for two years became a united nation, though Pinkie Cleugh was not far away.

The Battlefield Today

Peniel Heugh has a large Wellington monument on its summit and stands near the A68 a few miles north of Jedburgh.

Pinkie Cleugh/10 September 1547

English basinet, c1515, as used by Lord Grey's cavalry at Pinkie Cleugh (*Reproduced by permission of the Trustees of the Wallace Collection*)

The death of Henry VIII in 1547 did not alter the English policy of harrassment against Scotland. Lord Somerset, the Protector, during the minority of Edward VI, was forced to do something about the Scottish situation when they turned down his prosposals for a marriage between young Mary, Queen of Scots and King Edward. The Scottish Protector, James Hamilton, Earl of Arran, had much to contend with. The English held Broughty Castle and controlled the sea passage to Dundee. In Langholm on the Borders the English under Lord Wharton were being a perpetual nuisance and St Andrews Castle, under siege for some time by the Scots, was provisioned by English ships from Holy Island. The Scottish 'heretics' who held St Andrews, including the celebrated John Knox, finally surrendered

to a French fleet in July and, two months later, Somerset made up his mind to teach Scotland a lesson. The 'rough wooing' had begun in earnest.

The Battle

By the end of August the English army had arrived at Newcastle, consisting of nearly 18,000 men. It had 15 large cannon, 500 experienced cavalrymen under Lord Grey, 2,000 light horse under Sir Francis Bryan and 200 mounted arquebusiers under the Spanish mercenary Gamboa, whose men had been the first to use firearms at the Siege of Rhey in 1521. In between the infantry, equipped with sword and hackbut, were the archers. Few armies entering Scotland had ever been so well armed and they were well supported by Lord Clinton's fleet.

Arran's army was numerically stronger. He had 25,000 men of whom most were pikemen; the only cavalry was a small force of Border Horse commanded by Lord Home and his son. Arran took up a strong position near Inveresk with the River Esk protecting him from the English. On his left wing were the Highlanders under Angus; on his right he placed Lord Huntly and the Argyll archers and Home's cavalry. He commanded the centre. Opposite Somerset placed Lord Grey on the right wing, then the centre under Lord Warwick and finally Bryan's

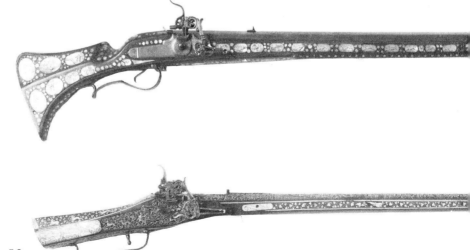

A sixteenth-century arquebus (*Reproduced by permission of the Trustees of the Wallace Collection*)

horse was on the left wing. Lord Clinton's fleet at Musselburgh were so placed that their guns protected the bridge over the Esk. On 9 September the Scots suffered a loss when their horse made a sortie and were cut down by the heavier English horse. Lord Home's son was captured and henceforth the Scots horse took no part in the battle. The Earl of Home himself was very badly wounded.

Somerset noticed that Inveresk Hill covered the Scots' position and that if he could occupy it with his guns he would probably succeed in covering the Scottish camp. Next morning in three columns the English headed for Inveresk Hill, crossing the Pinkie burn on the way. Mistaking this for a retreat to their ships, the Scots crossed the Esk and headed for Fawside Hill. The Scots infantry under Angus were equipped with eighteen-foot-long spears and formed squares to deal with the English horse, the first rank kneeling, the second sloping forward and the third standing. The charge of Lord Grey's horse was stoutly resisted by these spearmen and Lord Grey was wounded in the mouth and many of his men killed. Sir Andrew Flammock lost the Royal standard staff but saved the colours.

Gamboa's arquebusiers saved the day. Galloping forward they fired at Angus's men; with archers, cannon and Sir Peter Mewtas's hackbuteers attacking them,

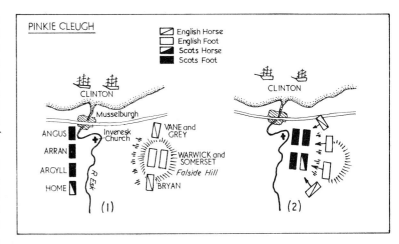

Angus's men had had enough. They retreated on Arran's infantry and forced the Scottish line back. A mass exodus from the Scottish position now started and the English ships took their toll by firing at the Roman bridge. In this way the Lord Fleming and the Masters of Buchan, Ogilvy, Erskine and Livingstone perished—all were sons of Earls. Some 1,500 prisoners were taken including the Earl of Huntly. Somerset lost few men, the most important being Shelley, commander of the Boulogne Horse.

Results

Somerset did not follow up his victory and Arran retreated to Stirling. The English fortified Haddington, burnt Leith and occupied the islands in the Forth, but at the Treaty of Boulogne in 1550 the English possessions were surrendered. Mary went to France and married the French Dauphin Francis. Somerset's 'rough wooing' achieved nothing.

The Battlefield Today

The best position for viewing this is from Inveresk Church; Fawside Hill can be clearly seen. The bridge at Musselburgh is still there, though used now for pedestrians only. In England there is a monument at Bunbury, Cheshire, to Sir George Beeston who died at the age of 102 and fought gallantly 'contra Scots apud Musselborrow'. There is no monument.

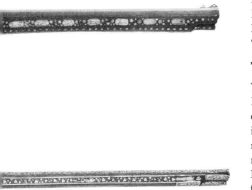

Newburn Ford/28 August 1640

Alexander Leslie, the Scottish commander at Newburn Ford (*Radio Times Hulton Picture Library*)

The First Scots War ended with an uneasy truce at Berwick and the Second started with the Scottish army under Leslie crossing the Tweed. Lord Conway, who commanded the garrison at Newcastle, attempted to fortify the river at Newburn to prevent the Scots encircling the town. He built two sconces there to cover the ford, accessible at low tide. His army was inexperienced and money was so short that the soldiers' pay had to be reduced to pay for their equipment. However he had 1,500 horse under Lord Wilmot and 3,000 foot to stop Leslie.

The Battle

Colonel Lunsford's regiment occupied one of the sconces and when, on 28 August, a single Scottish rider approached the ford, he was shot down by one of Lunsford's men. Leslie had arranged his cannon out of sight of the English army and had even put two of his leather guns on Newburn church tower. They opened fire and by clever shooting both sconces were destroyed, the defenders of the nearest being forced back.

At 4.0 p.m. the Edinburgh volunteers under Lord Hope's son crossed the river and drove the defenders out of the remaining sconce. Colonel Blair's musketeers and the Scottish horse followed and Conway gave permission for Wilmot's cavalry

The reign of Charles I was fraught with trouble from the first. Archbishop Laud's new prayerbook was not well received in Scotland and led to the signing of the Covenant and the First Bishops' War. The Scots had a capable general, Sir Alexander Leslie, a former field marshal to Gustavus Adolphus. He trained his men to fight in brigades with musketeers supporting the pikes. His cavalry was not strong but he had some heavy cannon and he developed the 'leather' cannon idea of the Swedish. The barrels were made of bar iron bound in hide and two could be carried on a single packhorse. They did not last long but could be mounted in unusual places.

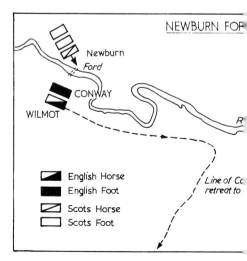

NEWBURN FOR[D]

Newburn Ford

CONWAY

WILMOT

R[

Line of C[o]
retreat to

English Horse
English Foot
Scots Horse
Scots Foot

to attack. The Scottish horse reeled but Blair's flank fire knocked down Wilmot's standard bearer, Charles Porter, and the standard was captured. Wilmot was forced back, some of his troopers riding over their infantry. About fifty were killed on both sides but the horse escaped to Durham and the foot to Newcastle, which surrendered on Leslie's approach. With Leslie was the young Montrose, getting his first taste of war. He was impressed with Leslie's control of his troops, who were not allowed to loot Newcastle. The coal trade carried on undisturbed and eventually Charles had to agree to buy off the Scots for a sum of £200,000. They left in August 1641, by which time Wilmot and others were more concerned with the growing struggle between King and Parliament.

The Battlefield Today

A disappointing battlefield to visit, Newburn is an industrial suburb of Newcastle. The river's course altered in the last century and no fords remain; one must have been near the present bridge. There is a tumulus at Ryton near the church but it may date from an earlier period than the Bishop's War. The Stella breastworks were visible until 1917 when they were destroyed. In the Black Gate museum at Newcastle there is a cartwheel found at Newburn, possibly from a cart that did not make the ford crossing, but there are no relics of the battle.

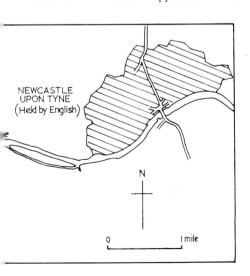

NEWCASTLE
UPON TYNE
(Held by English)

N

0   1 mile

59

Edge Hill/23 October 1642

Prince Rupert at Edge Hill

Edge Hill today (*author*)

The Civil War in 1641–6 was essentially a local war. Most county levies refused to cross county borders and there were parts of England—Norfolk and Suffolk for instance—where there was little action at all. The important battles took place in central England, because most of eastern and southern England was under Parliamentary control and most of the northern and western parts under Royalist control. There were important exceptions like Plymouth and Lyme held by Parliament, and initially towns like Reading and Buckingham were for the King.

The arms and tactics used were introduced by those with experience of

in a bandolier. Their muskets were long and heavy and had to be fired on a rest; they were inaccurate with a range of only about four hundred yards. Artillery was varied. The light guns—sakers, minions and falconets—were of very small bore and fired a three-pound ball. Heavier siege cannon, used at the Siege of Newark for example, were effective in making a breach but were very immobile and all Meldrum's heavy guns were captured after Newark, thereby adding to the significant defences of the town.

The King raised the Royal standard in Nottingham in August 1642. The fact that it blew down shortly afterwards was seen as an ill omen by some. He then proceeded to Shrewsbury gathering his army. With the Welsh infantry he had about 12,000 men, 3,000 of which were cavalry and dragoons. Lord Essex left London with the London-trained bands and an army of about the same size, but with less cavalry. He occupied Worcester and the Royalist army set off towards London on 12 October bypassing Essex, so that on the evening of 22 October Charles was at Edgecott when Essex was at Kineton. The opening shots of the Civil War had already been fired at Powick Bridge near Worcester, where some of Rupert's cavalry chased off a party of Fiennes's horse, out to intercept some silver plate being sent to Aberystwyth for the King's funds.

The Royalist army withdrew from the steep Edge Hill to the village of Radway, where the ground was more suitable for their cavalry. Rupert took the position of honour on the right wing; the centre was commanded by the Earl of Lindsey, who had little authority over Rupert and the left wing of horse was commanded by Lord Wilmot. Opposite, the Parliamentary horse was divided into four commands: Fielding, Balfour and Stapleton were on the right facing Wilmot and on the left was Commissary General Ramsey with his horse. The Royalist guns were in Battleton Holt (near where the present monument stands), covering Essex's march from Kineton towards Radway.

fighting on the continent. Thus Prince Rupert introduced the Swedish cavalry methods of Gustavus Adolphus. Instead of using the out-of-date caracole—by which the cavalry approached the enemy, let off a barrage of pistol fire, wheeled and returned to its starting point—he trained his troops to bunch together and break through the enemy lines, chasing them off the field. Those cavalrymen of his with no pistols were armed with pole-axes. Infantry on both sides were armed with the eighteen-foot pike, useful in defence. Interspersed with pikemen were the musketeers, who carried twelve rounds each—a round being bullet and powder—

The Battle

Edge Hill started with an artillery duel. Then Rupert advanced with the King's Lifeguard as their commander, Lord Bernard Stewart, had asked permission to join in the charge instead of remaining with Sir John Byron in the reserve. On approaching Ramsey the troop of horse commanded by Fortescue, a Parliamentarian, suddenly fired their pistols into the ground and changed sides, but in the confusion some of them were killed as they forgot to remove their orange scarves. Ramsey's men fled in terror along with most of their supporting infantry. The Royalist's left wing was similarly successful and Wilmot chased Fielding off the field. Two Parliamentary regiments of horse were left however—Balfour's and Stapleton's; probably the hedges and trees had concealed them from Wilmot and Sir John Byron who had joined in the left wing attack. Balfour led his troop in a wide sweep through Nicholas Byron's brigade, one Welsh regiment taking to its heels, then veered left into Battleton Holt capturing, at least temporarily, the Royalist guns. Unable to find any nails to block the powder holes, Balfour's men cut the traces and killed the gunners, and then returned to their own lines, being fired on by Parliamentary guns by mistake on their journey.

Stapleton's horse attacked the Royal standard itself where the Royalist foot under Lindsey fought bravely, Lindsey himself being mortally wounded. A great struggle took place round the Royal standard. Sir Edmund Verney, the standard bearer, was killed, the standard captured and the Royalist cause looked grim until five troops of Rupert's horse returned to the field. Captain John Smith noticed a trooper riding off with the Royal standard; he charge and killed him and another trooper, single-handed, rescued the standard. The King knighted him the following day.

Both armies withdrew during the night, the Royalists up the hill and the Parliamentarians to Kineton. Next morning Essex was reinforced by 2,000 men under John Hampden and the King moved south to Banbury. Essex marched to Warwick with Rupert's cavalry harrassing his rearguard. The battle was a draw: the Royalists had lost about the same number of men as the Parliamentarians, but they had not beaten Essex. The road was open to London but Essex got there first and, although Rupert stormed Brentford capturing valuable arms and ammunition, the massed London-trained bands at Turnham Green were too daunting for the Royalists to attack. Winter was approaching and Charles returned to Oxford.

Edge Hill is important as the first large-scale battle of the Civil War. The Royalists learned to keep a reserve of cavalry

EDGE HILL

Kineton

N

RAMSEY

RUPERT

The Oaks

ESSEX

Kings Leys Barn

Radway

STAPLETON

Battleton Holt

BALFOUR

LINDSEY

Edge Hill

FIELDING

WILMOT

0   1 mile

Royalist guns
Royalist Horse
Royalist Foot
Parliamentary Horse
Parliamentary Foot

instead of committing it all in the attack; the Parliamentarians learnt to distinguish their own men from the enemy and recognised that there were snags in trying to direct an army from London. The Royalist commander of the army went to Lord Ruthven, but there was continual dissent between Rupert and other commanders and even the King himself eventually fell out with his nephew.

Edge Hill Today

Edge Hill lies north of Banbury on the B4086. There is a small roadside monument on the left after descending the hill and crossing two small level crossings. Much of the battlefield is WD property and is covered with brick bunkers. The best view on a fine day can be seen from the top of the Castle Inn at Ratley Grange on Edge Hill itself, and the tower is said to have been Charles's first headquarters before the battle. Some bullets and cannon balls have been found including two twenty-eight pounders which were probably from Charles's heavy guns, fired before they were captured by Balfour.

63

Bradock Down/19 January 1643

The Civil War in Cornwall was almost entirely a Royalist affair at first. The principal landowners were Royalists and the arrival of Sir Ralph Hopton and Sir John Berkeley, both professional soldiers, with some horse, encouraged Sir Bevil Grenvile, Sir Nicholas Slanning, John Trevanion, John Arundel and Lord Mohun to rally their tenants and supporters and come to Hopton's aid. Arms were short but fortunately three Parliamentary ships took shelter in Falmouth harbour, where they were overpowered by Hopton's men and some money and valuable arms were captured.

The Parliamentary forces based at Plymouth were commanded by the Earl of Stamford; watching Hopton was a Scottish professional soldier, Colonel Ruthen, who took his Plymouth garrison troops out to Liskeard, where they occupied Bradock Down, digging in near the church. The five guns Ruthen had were not in position before Hopton opened fire with his two small drakes. These two guns were well hidden in the gorse of

Boconnoc Park, then the property of Lord Mohun, and it was this surprise more than anything else that upset Ruthen. He was keen to do battle before Stamford arrived, due perhaps to personal rivalry.

The Battle

Hopton placed the Cornish foot under Grenvile in the centre and his horse and dragoons on the wings. He gave Lord Mohun the command of the rearguard and the Royalist army said their prayers. The action is described by Grenvile in a letter to his wife: 'I had the van, and so after solemn prayers at the head of every division I led my part away, who followed me with so great courage, both down the hill and up the other that it struck a terror in them, while the second (line) came up gallantly after me and the wings of the horse charged on both sides. But their (ie the Parliamentarian's) courage failed as they stood not the first charge of foot, but fled in great disorder.'

Grenvile's men killed 200 and captured many more. All the Parliamentary guns

Boconnoc Church (*author*)

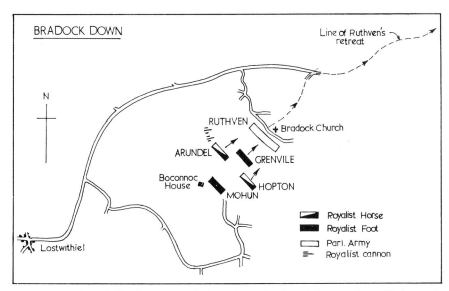

BRADOCK DOWN

Line of Ruthven's retreat

N

RUTHVEN
+ Bradock Church
ARUNDEL
GRENVILE
Boconnoc
House
HOPTON
MOHUN

Royalist Horse
Royalist Foot
Parl. Army
Royalist cannon

Lostwithiel

were captured and Ruthen escaped by boat from Saltash with difficulty. Bradock Down is an example of good follow-up work, for it cleared South Cornwall of the Parliamentary army until Essex's ill-fated expedition.

The Battlefield Today

The battlefield stands on private ground and there are so many trees that it is a confusing place to find. Bradock church is easily found by turning off the main Liskeard–Lostwithiel road at West Taphouse and climbing up a steep hill. This was the Parliamentary position. There are remains of earthworks at a nearby farm. The obelisk is nothing to do with the battle and the letters BS on the map refer to boundary stone not battle stone. The author was unable to find any monument and Captain Fortescue, owner of Boconnoc, could not help.

Boconnoc House, the Royalist headquarters (*author*)

65

The battle memorial high on the wall of the Tree Inn (*author*)

After Bradock Down and the Parliamentary retreat from Cornwall, Hopton realised that he had not the necessary strength to defeat the Plymouth garrison, which could be replenished by sea from London. After a temporary peace James Chudleigh, the young son of Sir George Chudleigh, took command of Stamford's army and succeeded, after failing to capture Launceston, in winning a skirmish at Sourton Down on 25 April, where he captured 1,000 muskets and all Hopton's correspondence in a successful ambush on the Royalist vanguard.

Encouraged by this, the Earl of Stamford at last took the field and moved into North Cornwall, camping at Stratton on a hill partly enclosed in ancient earthworks, some of which still stand today. Stamford had 6,800 men and could well afford to send his cavalry to Bodmin to prevent the trained bands from joining the Royalists. Hopton had about half this number, but his men were to prove that numbers did not count when it came to storming a defended position.

The Battle

Hopton set out from Launceston, determined to drive Stamford, whose army was now reduced to 5,400, out of Cornwall. He used the Tree Inn at Stratton as his headquarters and, dividing his army into four groups, he gave Sir John Berkeley command of the northern group, Sir Bevil Grenvile the western, Sir Nicholas Slanning the eastern and he himself took command of the southern group. The small band of Royalist horse under Digby commanded the road to Bideford. The first Royalist attacks were unsuccessful as the Parliamentary cannon commanded the attacking routes and James Chudleigh was a competent commander—Stamford seems to have left much of the work to him. By three o'clock in the afternoon Hopton sent a message to his field commanders that, owing to the shortage of ammunition, the position must be pressed by pike and sword. The remaining Parliamentary horse under Stamford himself decided to get out before it was too late and escaped to Bodmin. Chudleigh, his men frightened by the silent approach, led a desperate charge out of the position against Grenvile and Berkeley, who had the easiest route, but although making some impression, he took his men too far and was surrounded and captured. The remaining Parliamentarians huddled in the earthworks and Grenvile and Berkeley, now joined by Hopton, turned the captured Parliamentary cannon on the earthworks and forced the defenders to rush down the hill behind in the wake of their retreating cavalry. Some of them were caught by Slanning's men and others chased off by Digby. Some 1,700 prisoners were taken including Chudleigh, who joined the Royalists, and thirty officers, all the cannon and ammunition—seventy powder barrels—as well as £5,000 of coin. The Parliamentary cavalry in Bodmin escaped to Plymouth but its leader, Sir George Chudleigh, resigned his commission because of his son's behaviour. Stratton was probably the most remarkable Royalist victory in the Civil War but it brought Hopton in direct confrontation with Waller, a commander of a different calibre.

66

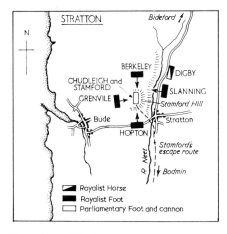

STRATTON

Bideford

CHUDLEIGH and STAMFORD
BERKELEY
GRENVILE
DIGBY
SLANNING
Stamford Hill
Bude
Stratton
HOPTON
Stamford's escape route
R. Neet
Bodmin

◨ Royalist Horse
■ Royalist Foot
☐ Parliamentary Foot and cannon

Stratton Today

The battlefield is easily found by taking the road up Stamford Hill towards Poughill from the main Bideford–Bude road (A39). After passing the Stamford Hotel, there is a seat by the side of the road, opposite which is Bevill House, which is the top of the hill. A little gate in the bank to the left of the house leads to the earthworks, where there is an arch and a new plaque to commemorate the battle. The land on the other side of the arch is private. The old memorial is high up in the side of the Tree Inn and reads: 'In this place the army of the rebels, under the command of the Earl of Stamford, received a signal overthrow by the valour of Sir Bevil Grenvile and the Cornish army on May 16, 1643'. Inside the inn are some scythes, said to have been used in the battle, and in the courtyard is a large portrait of local hero, Antony Payne, a seven-foot giant who fought in this battle and at Lansdown.

The battle monument (*author*)

Lansdown Hill/5 July 1643

Stratton broke the Parliamentary hold on Cornwall and part of Devon, leaving the route open for the Cornish army under Hopton and now reinforced by Prince Maurice's horse, towards Somerset. In Chard on 4 June the Royalists had 4,000 foot, 800 horse and dragoons, and 21 guns. Against them was Waller, whose army was smaller but had recently been reinforced by Sir Arthur Heselrig's regiment of 'Lobsters', so called because of their enclosing armour. Hopton moved to Bradford-on-Avon where Waller at Bath threatened him. On 10 June there was a cavalry action at Chewton Mendip where Maurice was slightly wounded and, for a time, captured, but the Earl of Carnarvon's regiment rescued him and beat off the enemy.

Waller drew up his army at Claverton Down (near Bath University) and Hopton sent Maurice to capture Claverton Bridge. Waller withdrew to Lansdown Hill and on 4 July Hopton camped at Marshfield.

The Battle

Next morning he approached Lansdown but realised Waller had found a very good position with his infantry behind stone breastworks and with his artillery trained on the approaching Royalists. Hopton, who divided his command with the Marquis of Hertford, a Cavalier leader of equal standing, decided to withdraw, which was a difficult manoeuvre under fire. Waller chased him with his horse, beating his rearguard at Cold Ashton, but a Cornish infantry regiment turned round and gave them a hot reception. Richard Atkyns, whose account of the battle is one of the best, attacked with Lord Arundel and Hertford's horse: 'we charged together, and both of us fell upon the commander-in-chief, and hurt him so, that he reeled and wheeled off, and the party with him'.

Carnarvon's horse was sent forward to aid the Cornish infantry, and Slanning and his musketeers attacked the Roundhead dragoons who were lining the hedges and woods and causing casualties. Hopton, whose headquarters was on Freezing Hill, sent Sir Bevil Grenvile and his pikemen up the hill to attack Waller's infantry with Carnarvon and Maurice's horse in between the infantry and musketeers. Waller's guns took great toll and some of the Royalist horse fled, going as far as Oxford believing the day to be lost.

The surviving horse charged five times and eventually the Royalist guns came into action, breaking down the Roundhead breastworks. Grenvile's men, supported by musketeers and some of the Cornish horse, pressed on and carried the Roundhead position, Grenvile himself being struck down in the moment of victory. His son was placed on Antony Payne's shoulders and the Cornish did not hesitate in their forward thrust.

The Roundheads retreated to another defensive wall and both sides camped for

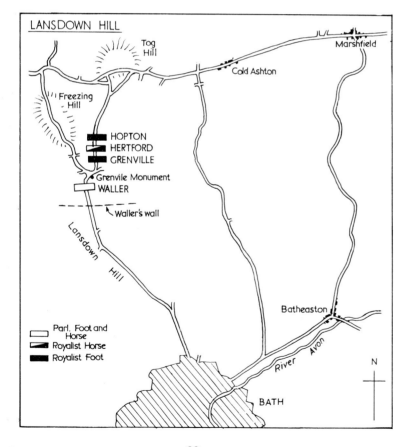

LANSDOWN HILL

Tog Hill
Marshfield
Cold Ashton
Freezing Hill
HOPTON
HERTFORD
GRENVILLE
Grenvile Monument
WALLER
Waller's wall
Lansdown Hill
Batheaston
River Avon
N
BATH

☐ Parl. Foot and Horse
◣ Royalist Horse
◼ Royalist Foot

the night on the battlefield. Waller arranged pikes and fires in his position and pulled off his men secretly, one regiment at a time, to Bath. Hopton paid a soldier a handsome sum to go forward and see what was happening. He was content to allow Waller to escape. His ammunition was very short and his army tired. A great tragedy then hit the Royalist army, for some Parliamentary captives were sitting in an ammunition cart and one lit a match to light a pipe. The cart blew up injuring Hopton (and presumably killing the captives) in the eyes. He survived but in the ensuing battle at Roundway Down he was in no state to play any part. In spite of winning Lansdown, fate was the real winner, and though the Royalists resumed their march on Oxford they still left Waller with a great part of his army intact behind them.

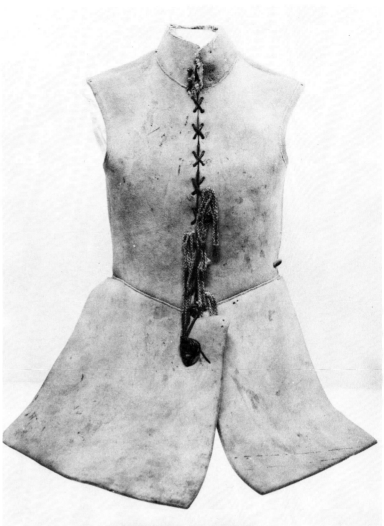

Sir Bevil Grenvile's monument
(*author*)

The Battlefield Today

A large monument to Sir Bevil Grenvile (spelt Granville on the stone) stands to the left of the road up Lansdown from the main Chippenham–Bristol road (A420). Further on the map shows 'earthworks' which may well have been Waller's final stonewall defence. From many aspects the battlefield is not greatly altered; the effect of musket balls on the stone must have caused considerable casualties.

A Roundhead buff coat, similar to those worn by Waller's men at Lansdown (*National Army Museum*)

69

Roundway Down/13 July 1643

Cavalier soldiers showing typical dress and armour (*Mary Evans Picture Library*)

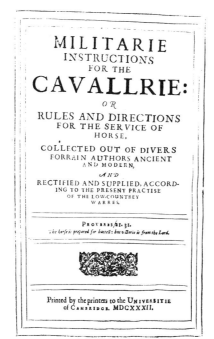

Title page from an early cavalry manual (*National Army Museum*)

The victory at Lansdown was a check on Waller, and Hopton's injury merely added to the Royalist difficulties. They were very short of ammunition and when they arrived at Devizes, Captain Pope went round collecting bedcord to make match. The following day, 10 July, Prince Maurice set out with the Marquis of Hertford and the cavalry to get help and munitions from Oxford, only 45 miles away. Waller, who had gathered reinforcements in Bath, had about 3,000 foot and 2,000 horse including Heselrig's 'Lobsters'. He soon reached Devizes and, positioning his army on Roundway Down, fired his cannon into the Royalist positions.

Help was on its way, however. In Marlborough the Royalist reinforcements gathered under Lord Wilmot; there were 1,800 horse divided into three brigades, commanded by himself and Maurice, Crawford and Sir John Byron. They had two small cannon to fire a pre-arranged signal to the waiting Hopton, whose Cornish foot were ready to take Waller in the rear.

The Battle

The old road from Marlborough went across the top of the Downs and when Maurice's force reached the foot of Morgan's Hill, they saw Waller begin to pull his army back to the Roundway–Beacon Hill position. Waller thought he could use Heselrig's heavy horse, which had already got the better of Crawford in a skirmish, to effect and, at the same time, keep an eye on the Royalist foot in Devizes. With Crawford as a reserve, Wilmot and Maurice took the right wing, Byron the left. The signal guns were fired and an answering puff came from Devizes castle. The Royalist forlorn hope commanded by Major Smith 'beat the Lobsters in the very body of their wing'. Confusion was caused by the retreating front rank running into the second and third ranks. Wilmot and Byron now charged. The enemy was twice their number but it seems the foot was left alone and both Parliamentary wings of horse were defeated. Slingsby watched from Devizes and said that 'on a sudden we could see the Enemy's whole body of horse face about and run with speed, and our horse in close body firing in their rear, till they chased them down the hill in a steep place where never a horse went down nor up before'.

Meanwhile the Cornish infantry led by Bassett and others climbed up Roundway Hill and attacked the Parliamentary foot who were threatened with their own cannon and forced to surrender. It was an amazing Royalist victory. Perfect co-operation between horse and foot with split second timing on Wilmot's part was the cause. Over 600 were killed and all Waller's guns, ammunition and baggage captured. Most of the Parliamentary leaders escaped, one of them saying that 'we must look upon this as the hand of our God mightily against us, for it was He that only made us fly'.

A few days later Bristol fell to Rupert and apart from Plymouth, Lyme and Poole, the west was in Royalist hands. 'Runaway Down' as the soldiers called it

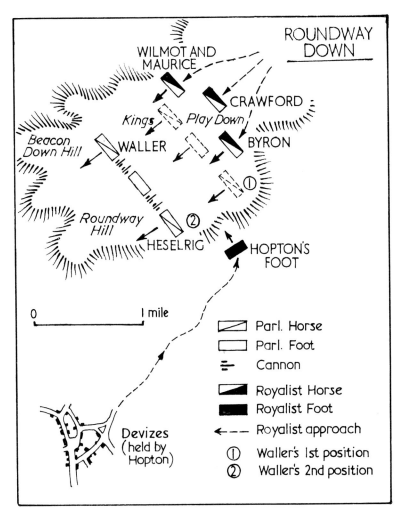

was a significant victory, but Charles now decided to relieve Gloucester and the defence there was made of sterner stuff than that at Bristol.

The Battlefield Today

Leaving Devizes by the A361, Roundway village is up the hill to the left just after Devizes barracks. Most of the land is now cultivated. The best view of the field is from King's Play Hill, reached from Heddington near Calne. The tracks are not suitable for cars but it is a walker's paradise. Devizes castle is privately owned and is not open to the public.

71

Newark/21 March 1644

The Queen's Sconce (*Major R. W. Naesmyth RA*)

A 2s 6d siegepiece coin from Newark (*Newark District Council Museum*)

Newark Castle (*author*)

By the beginning of 1644 both sides were anxious to gain help from untried sources. Charles looked to Ireland and Parliament looked to Scotland. The Marquis of Newcastle's Royalist forces in York were pressed both by the invading Scots and by the Parliamentarians in Hull; to relieve him from Oxford was a priority but the route to York passed through Newark. Here the Royalist garrison under Richard Byron was hard pressed by Sir John Meldrum, whose 6,500 men in March 1644 were centred on the Spittal, a house burnt the year before but positioned outside the Newark gate, where Byron with his water defences and forts was still holding out.

Prince Rupert was training new recruits at Shrewsbury and was ordered to Newark's relief. He collected two new regiments of Irish infantry under Colonel Tillier and the remains of Lord Byron's cavalry, recently defeated by Fairfax at Nantwich and, ferrying Tillier's men down the River Severn to Bridgnorth, he assembled his army there. Joining up with the Dudley Castle garrison he had about 6,000 men, most of them cavalry. By 20 March Rupert was at Bingham on the Nottingham–Grantham road. Early next morning Rupert took his horse through Balderton and occupied Beacon Hill,

leaving his infantry two miles behind struggling to catch up. Meldrum had his main force in the Island (the area north west of Newark surrounded by the rivers Trent and Devon) with Hobart's horse protecting the Spittal, but a bridge of boats at Winthorpe was the sole means of communication between the two groups.

The Battle

Rupert divided his horse into three groups. He personally led the right wing, Sir Richard Crane the left and Gerard his reserve with Lord Loughborough, who commanded the largest Royalist contingent. When he arrived, Tillier was instructed to attack Meldrum's bridge of boats over the Trent at Winthorpe from the north. It was an effective plan. The Royalist messenger who crossed at night into the town brought Byron the signal 'The big drum will be beaten in the morning'. By means of the Parliamentary garrison at Nottingham, Meldrum in fact had discovered that Rupert was advancing. He protected his bridge with cannon and, on the Island, his Nottingham regiment under Colonel King and the Norfolk redcoats defended Muskham bridge, which was a drawbridge protected by a sconce. Byron, presumably on Rupert's orders, took a large force of horse and infantry out to attack Muskham. The Norfolks fled burning the bridge behind them so that no one, not even the other Parliamentarians, could follow them.

Meanwhile an observer on Newark church spire was able to see Rupert's

cavalry charge three times. The first charge dislodged Thornhaugh who, badly wounded, was taken off to Nottingham in a cart. The second charge against Rossiter was more difficult; Rossiter placed his flank men six deep instead of three deep, so some got through to attack the reserve where Gerard was wounded and captured. His final charge cleared the area and Rossiter was forced to lead his remaining horse over the bridge.

Next morning Meldrum surrendered on fairly good terms, as his army was short of supplies. It was allowed to march out with personal belongings and the officers retained their swords, but Rupert captured the Parliamentary siege train, over 3,000 muskets and ammunition as well as many pikes and pistols. All these were handed to the hard-pressed Newark garrison. The Parliamentary outposts at Gainsborough, Lincoln, Sleaford and Crowland were over-run and the defences of Newark were so well constructed that they did not yield until May 1646 when the King crossed over to the Scots camp and the Governor, Lord Belasyse, was forced to surrender at the King's request.

Newark Today

Newark has a small museum in which there is an unfinished map of the siege-works, some cannonballs (mostly 30lb ones dragged from the river), a strange hackbut barrel with a 1in bore (presumably a fixed gun), a rusty sword and some interesting siege coins. By far the most unusual sight in Newark is the Queen's

Sconce, now adjacent to a car park and children's playground in Boundary Road. It is still in fairly good shape; each of the four angle bastions could have held two cannon, so that enemy attacking the town defences could also be fired on, and there was space for a regiment of foot to camp, if necessary in the centre dip, and protect the guns. The actual ditch surrounding it would have kept out cavalry, as would other pits filled with sharp stakes built in the Bannockburn tradition. A similar sconce, the King's Sconce built in 1615 on the site of the Spittal, lay to the north of the town adjacent to Malt Kiln lane. The original town wall can still be seen in part between Friary Road and Appleton Gate running along Sleaford Road. The castle is worth a visit and is best seen from across the river.

In the church is the monument to the Mayor of Newark, who for three nights running dreamt he was in a blazing house. When he removed his wife and family on the fourth day one of Meldrum's mortar shells hit the roof and set his house on fire.

More details of the personalities and defences of Newark in the Civil War can be found in *Newark on Trent, the Civil War Siegeworks* (HMSO, 1964).

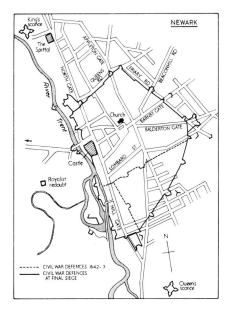

73

Cropredy Bridge/29 June 1644

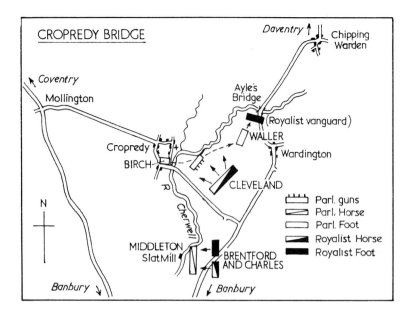

CROPREDY BRIDGE

Coventry
Mollington
Daventry ↑ | Chipping Warden
Ayle's Bridge
(Royalist vanguard)
WALLER
Wardington
Cropredy
BIRCH
CLEVELAND
N
Parl. guns
Parl. Horse
Parl. Foot
Royalist Horse
Royalist Foot
MIDDLETON
Slat Mill
BRENTFORD AND CHARLES
Banbury ↓
↓ Banbury

Hopton's defeat at Cheriton in the south reduced the power of Charles's forces in Oxford so both Reading and Abingdon were abandoned and their forces swelled those at Oxford. Prince Maurice was besieging Lyme and Oxford was almost

surrounded, with Essex at Abingdon, Waller at Newbridge on the Witney–Abingdon road and other Roundhead troops at Eynsham, Woodstock and Bletchingdon. Charles made one of his more active military decisions. He decided to break out and make for Worcester where he would be able to link up with the Royalist garrisons. However, when by 4 June he reached Bourton-on-the-Water, he heard that Essex's army had moved off to the Westcountry to relieve Lyme. Waller's army was at Banbury by the end of June and Charles, who had sent Rupert the message 'march with your whole strength to Worcester to meet me' if he failed to relieve York, was at Buckingham. Blocked at Banbury, Charles decided to move towards Daventry, and Waller—whose army was slightly smaller, about 6,000 to the Royalist's 7,500, two-thirds of which were horse—was also slowed down by his guns commanded by James Wemyss, previously a Royalist gunner. The River Cherwell kept the two forces at bay and Charles sent some horse ahead to hold Cropredy Bridge. Waller

The aime Levell by the mettall of the peece

The Levell Axis, or point blan

A page from a manual on the firing of cannon (*National Army Museum*)

74

knew of a ford a mile further south at Slat Mill so, sending Middleton's cavalry over the ford, he himself captured Cropredy Bridge from the other side, sending the Royalist horse to Ayle's Bridge a few miles north. He just managed to get his guns into position when the Royalists arrived.

The Battle

The Roundheads had divided their force into three; Waller himself was attacking the fleeing vanguard near Ayle's Bridge, Colonel Birch defended the bridge at Cropredy and Middleton had got bogged down at Slat Mill (near Williamscot House). The Earl of Northampton, a teenager but an experienced cavalry leader, led a series of charges that drove Middleton back over the river. Lord Cleveland, who commanded the main body of Royalist horse, charged Waller from the rear, capturing Wemyss and his guns on the way. The Roundheads were routed, Waller escaped with difficulty and only the redoubtable Birch kept the Royalist infantry off the bridge. Charles

himself directed his guns against Waller and by evening the Roundheads had gone. Waller's forces mutinied shortly after this battle and Charles was left with an open road to the west.

The Battlefield Today

Cropredy Bridge can easily be found off the A423 five miles north of Banbury. The present bridge is Victorian but not much larger than the old bridge; there is a plaque set in the parapet. Presumably the river was wider before the canal was built. The nearby cricket ground must have been a field used by the Royalist cavalry. In the church there is some of the Parliamentary armour and a short pike.

General Waller

75

Marston Moor/2 July 1644

Cromwell leading the Parliamentary forces (*Radio Times Hulton Picture Library*)

Lord Fairfax (*Radio Times Hulton Picture Library*)

(*opposite*) **The Marston Moor monument** (*author*)

In Spring 1644 the Marquis of Newcastle was besieged at York by Fairfax and Leven's Scottish army. In spite of Rupert's success at Newark, 27,000 Parliamentary forces were in the York area and it could only be a matter of time before Newcastle's garrison would be forced to surrender.

Prince Rupert, whose army had disintegrated after Newark since it consisted largely of garrison troops from towns as far apart as Ashby-de-la-Zouch and Dudley, went to Lancashire where by the end of May he had control of the Liverpool area including Stockport (captured 25 May) and Bolton (captured 28 May). He still had Tyldesley's Irish foot and Goring's horse and in Lancashire he gathered a considerable army of 18,000, over half of which were horse. By 26 June Rupert had reached Skipton and York was two days' march away. The Parliamentary forces were alarmed and, in order to stop Rupert joining the Marquis, all besieging forces drew out of their lines to Long Marston putting the River Nidd between them and Rupert. Rupert, remembering his success at Newark, devised a simple plan. He sent a large body of horse to Knaresborough as a decoy and with his main force he turned north and crossed the Ure at Boroughbridge and the Swale at Thornton Bridge. He still had the Ouse to cross to

get to York but at Poppleton he surprised and captured a bridge of boats commanded by some of Manchester's dragoons. He was now three miles from York and no one could stop him. By 1 July Newcastle and Goring, Rupert's Commander of Horse, were in conference and, in spite of Newcastle's warning to wait for further reinforcements, Rupert's plan for a battle was accepted. Meanwhile at Marston Moor the Scots had quarrelled with the English and Leven led his men off to Tadcaster. Water was short and there was a possibility that Rupert might strike from the south. As Clarendon pointed out 'The Prince had done his work and if he had sat still, the other great army would have mouldered'.

The Battle

Early next morning Rupert's army marched out to take up their positions at Long Marston. Facing them was Lord Fairfax's rearguard, considerably outnumbered as most of the large Scottish contingent (two-thirds of the Allied army) was still in Tadcaster. Rupert had to wait for Eythin, who was second in command of Newcastle's foot and whose men were permitted to raid the siege lines, to appear before he could get his army into position. It was arranged with Rupert and Byron's horse on the right, some of whom had been part of the advance guard from Knaresborough so were holding the ground furthest from York (ie on the right of the Long Marston–Tockwith road). Newcastle's Whitecoats held the centre and on the left Goring and Langdale had their horse. The Allied army had 25 pieces of ordnance and Rupert had more than that number, though less powerful. In fact the artillery played little part in Marston Moor which was essentially one of movement.

Fairfax placed Cromwell's horse on the left opposite Rupert, Manchester's foot next to them, then his own, next the Scottish foot under Baillie, and finally Thomas Fairfax and Lambert with their horse on the right. His army was in three lines unlike the Royalist's which, apart from the centre where Widdrington's reserve made a third line, was in two lines, but the Allies had command of the higher ground. The Allied line had to get over a ditch to attack the Royalists while on the right Sir Thomas Fairfax faced both ditch and hedge lined with musketeers, for Moor Lane was well defended. When at 7.0 p.m. the Allied line moved forward, Goring was ready for them, and his horse cut through the Allied horse chasing them from the field and his second line attacked the Scottish foot. Only Thomas Fairfax and a small contingent broke through. On the left Cromwell was wounded in the initial charge and taken off to have his wound dressed at Tockwith. Rupert's men stood firm at first but were gradually outnumbered, and Leslie's horse chased them off the field, so that at about 8.30 p.m. all the generals were absent—even Lord Fairfax had gone home to Cawood, believing the day lost. However Crawford, Manchester's second-in-command, held his own against Newcastle and Eythin, and Cromwell, returning from Tockwith, was reinforced by Thomas Fairfax who, though wounded, had managed to ride round the back of the Royalists to his own lines unrecognised. The Parliamentary army was in disarray but at least Tom Fairfax and Cromwell made a plan, whereas in the Royalist army there was no overall commander—Rupert being off the field and Newcastle hemmed in with his infantry which was now to be attacked from the rear. Cromwell, guided by Tom Fairfax, took his Ironsides round the back of the Royalists and drove off Goring from the rear, then attacked the White-coats who were driven into White Syke Close. They refused to surrender and by next morning most of them had been killed or wounded.

Aftermath

Marston Moor was one of the most confused battles fought in the Civil War. Some 4,500 were buried the next day and of this number at least 3,000 were Royalists,

many of them gentlemen. Rupert managed to extricate most of his horse and returned to Chester. Newcastle, distressed by the defeat, took ship for Holland and Sir Thomas Glenham, an old experienced soldier, was forced to surrender York on 16 July. Cromwell was made General of Horse and Rupert lost his reputation; perhaps these two results were the most important consequences of this battle.

1 Rupert
2 Eythin
3 Goring
4 Widdrington
5 Cromwell and Leslie
6 Manchester
7 Lord Fairfax
8 Baillie
9 Thomas Fairfax
The Parliamentary army was arranged in three lines, the Royalist army in two lines

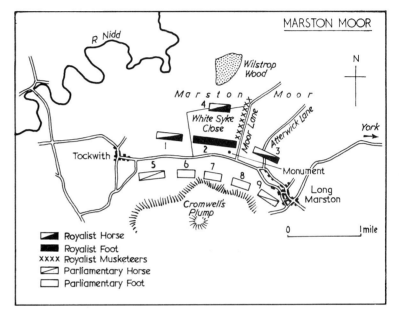

Marston Moor Today

The village of Long Marston is some nine miles out of York on the B1224. There is a large monument beside the road, at the end of Moor Lane where Tom Fairfax made his fatal charge. Opposite is 'Cromwell's Plump', a few trees on a small hill, where the Parliamentary chaplin Ashe sat and watched the battle. In York Museum there is a model of the battle and a few relics.

Lostwithiel/2 September 1644

After his victory at Cropredy Bridge, Charles pressed on into the Westcountry. Essex, with 8,000 foot and 2,000 horse, was in a quandary after relieving Plymouth, for he could either turn back and fight the King, with the knowledge that the Cornish army was in his rear, or he could turn on the Royalists and press harder on Cornwall, with the hope that the Parliamentary fleet under Warwick would be there to rescue him from Falmouth or Fowey. However the wind was against Warwick sending help from Plymouth—it seems that there was also a sense of bitterness between Warwick and Essex, the former being disinclined to send food to Essex's army that he had paid for and was needed by his troops in Plymouth.

By 7 August Essex was surrounded at Lostwithiel. Charles set up his headquarters at Boconnoc in Lord Mohun's attractive home (*see* Bradock Down, p 64) and Grenvile's foot occupied Bodmin before storming Restormel Castle, where Weare's Devonshire Regiment retreated without a fight, such was the reputation of the Cornish Royalist foot. Maurice and Brentford occupied Druid's Hill and Beacon Hill to the east of Lostwithiel, and blocked the Lostwithiel–Plymouth road. Goring, who had replaced Wilmot as Lieutenant-General of Horse, was ordered to capture Par and St Blazey.

Essex hoped for help from Middleton's army, which had been despatched by Parliament to relieve him. On 14 August however 2,000 men under Middleton were defeated by Sir Francis Doddington near Sherborne. In the early hours of 31 August Balfour took the Parliamentary cavalry silently out of Lostwithiel, avoided a cottage full of Royalist musketeers, and made for Saltash. Chased by Lord Cleveland, 100 men were killed or captured, but Balfour arrived safely in Plymouth with the other 1,900.

The Battle

There was continuous skirmishing throughout the Lostwithiel campaign, but it was a strategic manoeuvring for position rather than a pitched battle. The weather was against Essex, who now retreated to Castle Dore with his foot. 'The ways were so extreme foul,' he wrote, 'with excessive rain and the harness for the draught horses so rotten as that in the marching we lost three demi-culverins and a brass piece . . . thirty horses were put to each of these yet we could not reach them.'

Bassett led Grenvile's foot against the Roundheads' flank at Castle Dore. Essex

LOSTWITHIEL

Lanhydrock (occupied by Grenvile) 12 August

(occupied by Grenvile) 21 August

Restormel Castle

David's Hill

Balfour's escape route - 31 August

N

MAURICE

Musketeers

Beacon Hill

Boconnoc House

CHARLES HQ

LOSTWITHIEL

BRENTFORD

Parliamentary Horse
Parliamentary Foot
Royalist Horse
Royalist Foot
Royalist strongpoints

Lervyn Wood

Clift

NORTHAMPTON

GRENVILE

ESSEX

St Blazey

BUTLER
BARTLET

Castle Dore

WEARE

St Veep

GORING

R Fowey

Par Sands

Bodinnick

FOWEY

Polruan

0   1 mile

attempted a counter-attack but his men were weary, starved and unwilling to fight. The Devon men retreated again followed by both Butler's and Bartlet's regiments, and the road was open for the Royalists. Essex now decided to escape. It was a Dunkirk situation with no ships. but there was a small fishing boat and, seizing this, Essex left with Lord Robartes, whose house at Lanhydrock was captured by the Royalists, and Sir John Merrick, to Plymouth. Skippon was left to arrange a retreat. He had consulted Essex and made plans for a further stand at Menabilly, but his army was too weak and his ammunition too low to do so. When he got to London, Essex blamed Weare, Butler and Bartlet for his defeat.

The Surrender

After a parley on 1 September, Skippon's tired men laid down their arms on 2 September. A total of 6,000 surrendered; presumably there were some who escaped but the local people were pro-Royalist and the long files of prisoners, who were allowed to march to Portsmouth, had to be escorted out of Cornwall by Royalists to prevent them being attacked by the Cornish. Charles captured 42 guns, a mortar and 5,000 stand of arms. The

Parliamentary regiments kept their colours and were allowed one wagon each. Nevertheless food was so scanty that by the time they reached Portsmouth, escorted by Middleton's horse, their numbers had dwindled to less than 4,000 through sickness and desertion. What was surprising was Charles's treatment of the officers. He allowed them to go. Skippon, in particular, was to play a notable part in training the New Model Army at Reading, and also at Naseby. Why he, Butler, Weare and Bartlet were not imprisoned in Cornwall is difficult to understand, but war in the seventeenth century was still a chivalrous affair and prisoners were an expense that the holding army did not deem worthwhile.

Lostwithiel Today

There are three particular places to see at or near Lostwithiel: Lord Robarte's house at Lanhydrock is famous for its garden and is open to the public (*see* National Trust leaflets), Castle Dore on the B3269 Lostwithiel–Fowey road is in good condition and Restormel Castle, owned by the Department of the Environment, is a splendid example of a shell keep and is well worth a visit.

The Fowey estuary and Polruan fort which was held by the Royalists (*author*)

The Earl of Essex (*Radio Times Hulton Picture Library*)

Restormel Castle (*J. MacCormack*)

Newbury/28 October 1644

There were two battles at Newbury. The first was a Royalist success in some respects but neither army was in the field. It was a hedge fight, lasting all day on 20 September 1643 and apart from the death of Lucius Cary, Lord Falkland, who has a memorial near the Gun Inn, there is little to see of where the action took place. Essex's army got through to London but was badly mauled by the Royalists, who ran out of powder at the end.

The second battle of Newbury is easier to follow, and the two main strongpoints, Donnington Castle and Shaw House, are much as they were in 1644, the former being now a ruin. It is also a most interesting battle in that it was fought on two fronts and that the artillery played a considerable part.

After his success at Lostwithiel, Charles determined to relieve his hard-pressed garrisons at Basing House, Donnington and Banbury. The latter was left to the Earl of Northampton; Basing House was pressed by three armies under Manchester, Waller and Essex, whose cavalry had escaped from Lostwithiel. On 18 October the Royalist cavalry got the better of Waller's horse in Andover, and advanced as far as Kingsclere. The uncertain Parliamentary leaders suspected that the King had designs on Reading

Donnington Castle: the Royalist earthworks are visible in the foreground

and moved their army to Swallowfield, between Basingstoke and Reading. Charles however slipped into Newbury and relieved the gallant Colonel Boys at Donnington.

Essex was ill and consequently did not influence the Parliamentary decision to attack the Royalists at Donnington on two fronts. Manchester with the artillery positioned his foot on Clay Hill between Thatcham and Newbury; Waller with the horse under Skippon, Cromwell and Balfour and some foot as well as light cannon left on 26 October by a circular route, involving a night in the open at Chieveley, via Hermitage and Boxford to attack Charles at Speen. Colonel Hurry, or some other turncoat, gave information of the Parliamentary scheme to Charles who put his Cornish foot and Maurice's horse into Speen. A breastwork was built with five cannon commanding the road from the west and Boys' guns at Donnington were all trained on the route of the Parliamentary approach. Meanwhile at Shaw House Astley and Lisle's foot were well positioned to withstand an attack from Clay Hill. Massive banks of earth surrounded the house, which seems to have been a Royalist outpost before the battle, probably fortified by Colonel Boys.

The Battle

The second battle of Newbury was in itself two battles. The tired combined army of Skippon and Waller did not reach the Royalist blockade to the west of Newbury until 5.0 p.m., by which time it was getting dark. They attacked with spirit and the breastwork was captured together with its guns, which the Lostwithiel survivors recognised as their former property. The outposts of Donnington gave way, but the Castle still remained in Royalist hands. Charles sent the Earl of Cleveland's brigade to help Maurice and Goring, and Boys kept Cromwell, strangely subdued, at bay. Finally Skippon withdrew his men as the darkness made all recognition difficult.

The signal Manchester had expected

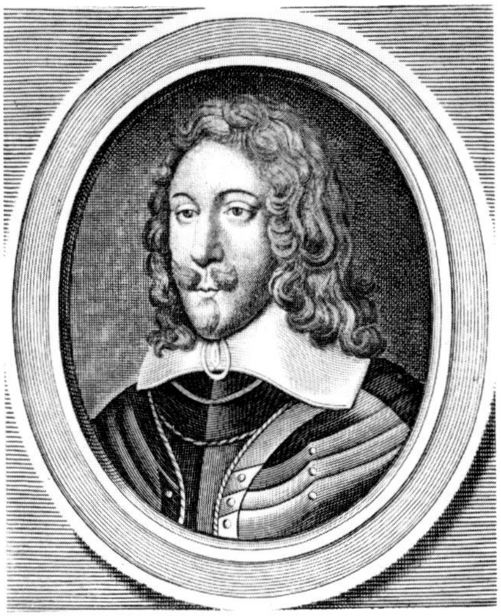

The second Earl of Manchester (*Radio Times Hulton Picture Library*)

from Speen telling him when to attack was never heard and by the time his two columns moved down the hill, one to attack Shaw village, the other the house, darkness made communications difficult. There was a great deal of hand-to-hand fighting round Shaw house and even, at one point, in the garden. The Royalist guns and the musketeers in the dry moat took care of this attack and eventually it broke up. In the village Sir George Lisle, stripped to his shirt for easy recognition in the dark, attacked the other Parliamentary column with both horse and foot. Five hundred men were killed in one spot and with cries of 'Beware the white witch' the men of Manchester's regiment retreated in dismay.

During the night Charles decided to withdraw while he still had the time. Perhaps he should have attacked again but he was anxious to get to Bath where Rupert was waiting with reinforcements and he had the safety of the young Prince of Wales, who was with him, to consider. The wounded, stores and guns were left with Boys in the Castle and the army moved silently out towards Wallingford, where Maurice directed it safely to Oxford, the King and his party going to Bath. A week later 1,500 men returned under Prince Rupert, relieved Boys and recovered their artillery while a party under Colonel Gage relieved Basing House. Newbury II can be called a Royalist victory, but a hard-fought one.

Newbury Today

Leaving Newbury by the A34, Donnington Castle can be seen on the hill to the left. Its gatehouse is open to the public. On the other side of the A34 is Shaw House, now a school. In 1822 some skeletons were found when erecting new greenhouses on the north-east side of Shaw House. Kettle drums, armour, an iron cap and cloak said to have been worn by Cromwell were at one time in the house, as well as a bullet kept in a glass-case, said to have been fired at the King.

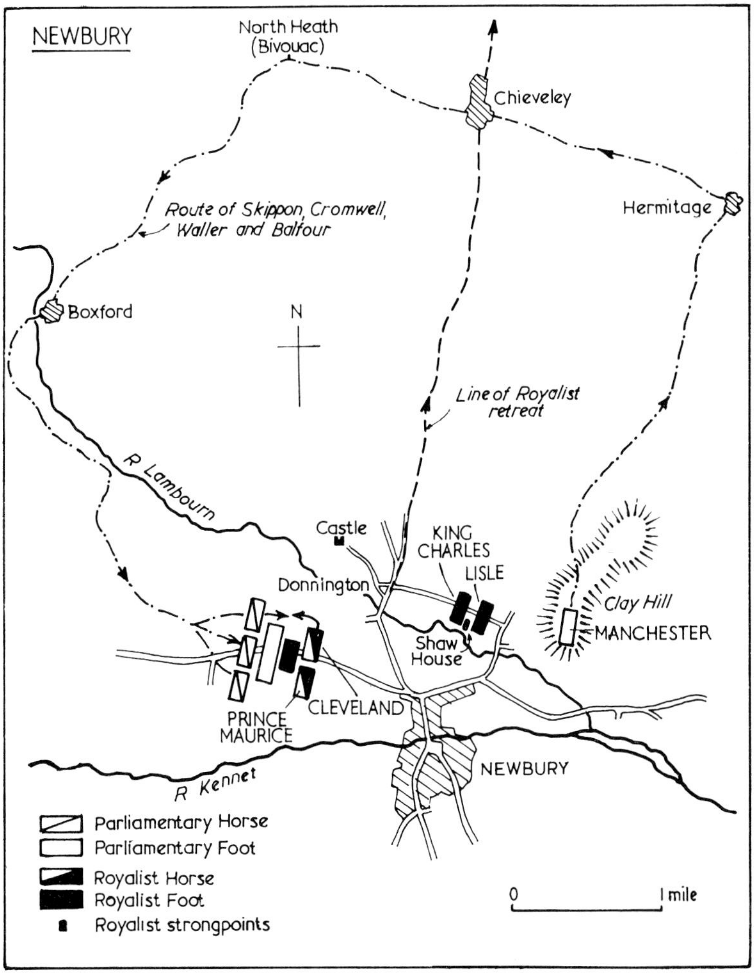
NEWBURY
North Heath (Bivouac)
Chieveley
Hermitage
Route of Skippon, Cromwell, Waller and Balfour
Boxford
N
Line of Royalist retreat
R Lambourn
Castle
Donnington
KING CHARLES
LISLE
Clay Hill
MANCHESTER
Shaw House
CLEVELAND
PRINCE MAURICE
NEWBURY
R Kennet
Parliamentary Horse
Parliamentary Foot
Royalist Horse
Royalist Foot
Royalist strongpoints
0
1 mile

Auldearn/9 May 1645

The battle of Marston Moor was a triumph for the Parliamentary cause. Two days after the battle Prince Rupert was at Richmond with the remains of the Royalist horse. Here he met the 32-year-old James Graham, Marquis of Montrose, Lieutenant-General of the Royalists in Scotland. Asking for 1,000 horse to get to Scotland he was refused any, but undismayed he travelled with two companions, disguised as a groom, until he reached Perth. He remained nearby until word came that the Marquis of Antrim had landed on the west coast with 2,000 men, mostly Macdonalds, for the Royalist army. Montrose met them at Blair Atholl, where they were joined by the Robertsons and Stewarts. At last he had an army.

In September 1644 Montrose defeated Lord Elcho (ancestor of Prince Charles's cavalry leader) at Tippermuir near Perth. It was a resounding victory but Montrose was still not strong enough to hold on to any town he captured. By 12 September he was on the outskirts of Aberdeen, where a Covenant army under Burleigh held the town. Montrose remembered Lord Kilpont, a friend as well as a useful supporter, who had been murdered in a quarrel, and may have been in an angry mood. At all events Aberdeen was not only captured but sacked and some hundred citizens killed. Argyll now entered Aberdeen after Montrose's departure with an army of 2,500 foot and 1,500 horse. Winter was approaching and Montrose took to the mountains. On 2 February 1645 Argyll's Campbells were caught and defeated at Inverlochy. Argyll himself escaped by boat but his army lost almost as many men as Montrose had under his command. The latter's Macdonalds had no love for Argyll's Campbells and the slaughter was excessive. Perhaps the Glencoe Massacre was part retaliation for Inverlochy.

Colonel Hurry, once a Royalist but now a Parliamentary cavalry leader, was sent

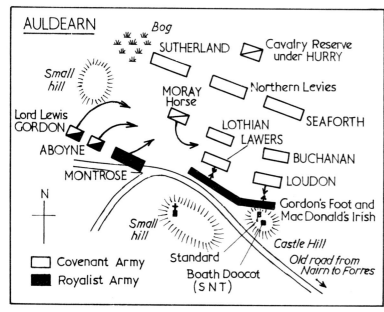

AULDEARN

Covenant Army

Royalist Army

with General Baillie to defeat Montrose. He was an experienced campaigner; when Montrose's weary army entered Dundee for supplies, Hurry nearly caught them there. By 8 May, Montrose was at Auldearn, between the valleys of Findhorn and Nairn. After carefully choosing his ground, Montrose placed his Irish under Alasdair Macdonald on the right wing, where the Boath Doocot stands on Castle Hill. On the left was his horse of about 200 men, inexperienced, and mostly Gordons who had fought against him at Aberdeen. Hurry had nearly 4,000 foot and 400 cavalry.

The Battle

The army under Baillie was burning Royalist crofts in Atholl and Hurry made no effort to wait for it, believing his army strong enough to deal with Montrose on its own. He was to be mistaken. Approaching Auldearn from the north he found that he could not deploy his men easily because of boggy ground on his right wing. In front were the Lawers Campbells and then the Northern Levies with Seaforth's foot; in the rear was his own trusty horse. Lawers and the Loudon foot attacked Alasdair's Irish on Castle Hill with the support of two further foot regiments under Lothian and Buchanan. In spite of fighting in their usual wild manner, the Irish were pushed slowly back.

Montrose was warned what was happening and, having concealed his cavalry, suddenly gave them the order to charge. 'Will you let Macdonald have all the glory of the day?' he said to young Lewis Gordon. The latter charged the Moray horse; their commander Major Drummond, in panic, gave the wrong order and they wheeled round colliding with the Lothian regiment. Aboyne's horse now attacked the foot regiments and the Northern Levies and Hurry's horse left the field without resistance. Hurry himself tried to stop the retreat but in the end escaped north with barely 100 horse. For fourteen miles the pursuit continued with Lord Gordon's men cutting down the Covenanters. Drummond was tried and shot as a traitor in Inverness.

Montrose's tactics of fighting with a weak right wing, no centre—all he had were a few musketeers in the village gardens—and concealing his cavalry were tactics that worked well. His Irish had fired when the enemy was nearly on them, a plan used by Murray at Falkirk, Dundee at Killiecrankie and by Cumberland at Fontenoy. The device of a weak right wing and an encircling left was used on a grand scale by Napoleon at Austerlitz to break the enemy centre. In England the news of Auldearn worried the Scots and Leven withdrew to Westmorland to

prevent Montrose from coming south. The Scottish Royalists and the English Royalists were still not strong enough to link up, however, and Montrose had Baillie's army to conquer.

The viewpoint at Auldearn
(*The National Trust of Scotland*)

Auldearn Today

The village is on the old Nairn–Forres road (A96), not the new one. The Scottish National Trust have made a viewpoint with a most helpful map and the Boath Doocot is well preserved. It is difficult to see how Montrose could have known what was happening on his right wing—presumably he had a series of messengers.

83

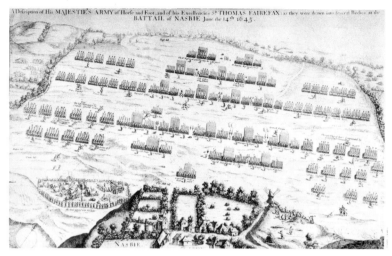

A contemporary plan of the battle (*National Army Museum*)

The Naseby obelisk (*The British Tourist Authority*)

plan, the Royalists had ten large cannon and the Néw Model ten, but artistic licence does not always prove accurate.

Fairfax drew up his army on Red Hill ridge with his right wing, Cromwell's horse, at New House Farm and on his left wing Ireton's horse, extending to Red Hill Farm. In the centre was Fairfax's foot, and Colonels Hammond, Rainsborough and Pride formed the reserve. One of the advantages of the New Model's positioning was that each division of cavalry was in two or only one squadron under one commander, unlike the Royalist tertias. If a commander was killed the

By the beginning of 1645 the Royalist position was precarious. They still controlled south-west England, where the siege of Taunton, held by Blake for Parliament, was nearly successful. In the same month, May, Rupert sacked Leicester and 140 carts of spoils were conveyed to Newark. Fairfax was made overall commander of the New Model Army which was established using Essex's old regiments as its core and Cromwell's Ironsides as its main cavalry arm. With proper pay, food and discipline, it was a great improvement on any previous Civil War army.

Moving south after Leicester's capture, some of the Royalist vanguard were captured sitting at a table in an inn in Naseby village (the table still exists in the church).

The Royalists were the first to position their army. Rupert discovered Dust Hill and he positioned his men, outnumbered two to one by the New Model Army, facing south with the wind in his favour so that smoke would drive in the enemy's faces. The Royalist front, a mile long, as usual had Rupert's cavalry on the right wing with Langdale's northern horse on the left. In the centre was Sir Jacob Astley's foot in three tertias—pikes in the centre and musketeers on each flank—and in the rear was Colonel Howard's horse, Rupert's foot and the King and his bodyguard. According to the Sprigge

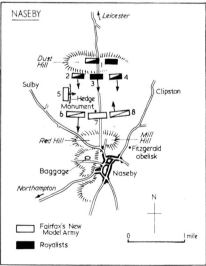

1 King
2 Rupert
3 Astley
4 Langdale
5 Okey
6 Ireton
7 Skippon
8 Cromwell

84

other two sections did not have to wander about with no orders. The Association horse, perhaps weaker than others, was divided into two divisions, one of the left wing and one on the right. Fairfax lined the Sulby hedge with Okey's dragoons on the left and in front Skippon's forlorn hope of 300 musketeers, probably volunteers, were placed to break up the Royalist flanks.

The Battle

To some extent Naseby was a repeat of Edge Hill with a flavour of Marston Moor. At about 10.0 a.m. Rupert's horse attacked in two waves and took all before them. Ireton was wounded in the thigh and captured; only Okey's dragoons prevented Butler's horse from being chased off the field. For two miles Rupert carried on the chase until he met the Parliamentary baggage train, where musketeers forced him back. In the centre Astley's foot pressed down on Skippon, some of whose new recruits fell back on the second line. Gradually the overwhelming numbers forced Astley's men into changing attack to defence but no ground was surrendered.

On the left wing Langdale attacked cautiously. The terrain was not too good for horse and there was a steep incline to Cromwell's position. Whalley's regiment charged down and broke up the front line of Langdale's horse, who fought back with their pistols. Some retreated to form up with Rupert's foot regiment and others, according to Clarendon 'fled farther and faster than became them'. Cromwell now wheeled to the left and attacked the Royalist foot. The King, seeing what was happening from his high viewpoint, proposed leading his lifeguards in a charge. There is a famous oil painting showing the Earl of Carnwath leading the King's horse round to prevent this; it was the signal of defeat. All surviving Royalist horse retreated off the field leaving the foot to cope as best they could. Astley's men laid down their arms, Rupert's bluecoats fought to the bitter end, and by lunchtime the battle was over.

Results

Fairfax won a resounding victory, capturing not only all the King's baggage, jewels and about £100,000 in gold and silver plate but, more important, all the Royalist foot. Cromwell closed his eyes to the slaughter of about 200 female camp followers, said to have been Irish women, and said Naseby was a great victory 'of which I had great assurance and God did it'. Eleven months later the First Civil War was over when Charles surrendered to the Scots near Newark.

Cromwell's charge at Naseby
(*Radio Times Hulton Picture Library*)

Naseby Today

One of the least spoilt of English battlefields, Naseby is easily found between Northampton and Market Harborough. A monument erected in 1936 supposedly shows where Cromwell charged. There is a large obelisk erected in 1823, not exactly on the battle site, that states the battle 'led to the subversion of the throne, the altar and the constitution . . . leaving a useful lesson to British kings never to exceed the bounds of their prerogative'. There is now a museum at Naseby only, alas, open at weekends.

After Auldearn, Montrose had to face Baillie, who blocked his road to the south. The Irish left his ranks to get recruits and, with his headquarters at Corgarff Castle, Montrose moved north to threaten Baillie at Keith. The latter had also been depleted of some of his troops, which had been sent to join another Covenanter, Lindsay, at Perth. Both armies were about the same size. Baillie had 1,200 foot and 500 horse under Balcarres. Montrose had less horse, but he divided it into two, putting the reserve under the Master of Napier and keeping his Gordon horse in the front line with his Highlanders.

Retreating south to the village of Alford,

Montrose set a trap for Baillie. The only way over the Don was across the Forbes ford and Montrose positioned his men on Gallows Hill near the crossroads at Ardgathen. He concealed his horse and made sure that only a part of his infantry would be visible to the oncoming Baillie. His right flank was protected by a bog and his left by the Leochel, a tributary of the Don.

The Battle

Montrose, recalling Newburn Ford, decided not to attack Baillie when he crossed the ford, but to wait until his army was all over. In this way he could catch

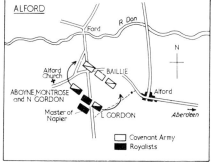

horse now charged on the left wing and Balcarres retreated back across the ford. Baillie's infantry was pressed on all sides and most died fighting.

Baillie escaped with Argyll and Balcarres and a few others. The young Lord Gordon was struck down from behind on his last charge; it was a sad army that made its way into Aberdeen, for young Gordon had been very popular. It made the Gordons even more bloodthirsty when they caught up with Baillie again and defeated him at Kilsyth. Shortly before Montrose won Alford, the King lost Naseby, so the result made little difference to the Civil War.

Alford Today

The village of Alford is modern; the old village was further west near the church. The view from Gallows Hill to the ford, now a bridge, is worth seeing. The Gordon stone, commemorating Lord Gordon, is railed off in a field outside the village. The crossed swords on the Ordnance Survey map is inaccurate as to the position of the battle.

Corgarff Castle, Montrose's headquarters; it was later adapted for military use after The '45 (*Aberdeen Journals Ltd*)

him retreating, for it is difficult to get over a narrow ford if an enemy is at your back and your foothold is insecure.

Balcarres decided to turn the enemy's flank by advancing to the left once over the ford, while Baillie came on slowly with his infantry. The young Lord Gordon recognised some of the cattle being driven over the ford by the enemy as his own; in a rage he charged down on Balcarres, but the latter fought back with his three squadrons of horse, outnumbering the Gordon horse. Nathaniel Gordon and his left wing foot turned the tide—they advanced with dirks drawn and stabbed the Covenanter's horses. The Aboyne

Philiphaugh/13 September 1645

An idyllically peaceful view of the battlesite; Leslie's troops came down the haugh near the farmhouse on the right (*Radio Times Hulton Picture Library*)

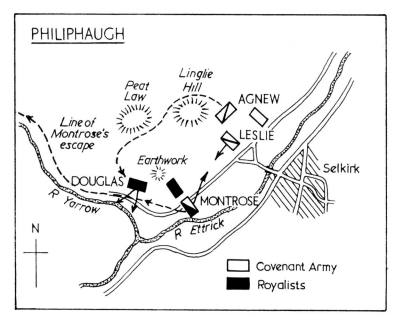

Montrose occupied Glasgow after Kilsyth, but as so often after his victories, his army dwindled. Aboyne went north with the Gordons and the Irish left for Galloway. With scarcely 700 men he left for the Borders hoping to collect troops to reinforce the English Royalists. General Leslie, then besieging Hereford, decided it was time to move north when he heard the news of Alford and Kilsyth. He had a well equipped army of 6,000, mostly horse, and he moved north by the east coast route. By September he was at Gladsmuir (near the battlefield of Prestonpans) when he was given information that Montrose was encamped outside Selkirk. On 12 September Montrose thought himself to be fairly secure by the junction of the Yarrow and Ettrick rivers. His scouts did not report anything though one, Charteris of Armisfield, arrived at midnight, having been driven out of Sunderland village by Leslie's vanguard. However, no-one woke Montrose in a house in Selkirk; it was too late. Early on 13 September Leslie approached the Royalist camp with one party of dragoons under Agnew on one side of the Ettrick and his main body on the other side.

The Battle

Perhaps the most effective raid of all is a dawn attack. In the early morning fog of 13 September, Montrose's men had little chance. The Irish were slaughtered; Montrose himself, collecting what few horsemen he could find, charged Leslie's horse but everywhere they were outnumbered. The shallow trenches dug by the Irish were not easy to defend and suddenly Agnew's dragoons attacked them from the other side. Retreat was the only hope and, with Crawford, the Napiers and a few others, Montrose escaped north. In April 1650 he was defeated again at Carbisdale and given up by Macleod of Assynt to the Covenanters, who tried him and executed him in Edinburgh. He was only thirty-eight when he died.

The Battlefield Today

Two miles west of Selkirk just off the A708 is the monument to Philiphaugh. It stands in private grounds near a tennis court and is in memory of 'the Covenanters who fought and gained the Battle' rather than the Royalists. Nearby on the other side of the river is Newark Castle where the Irish prisoners and camp followers were slaughtered after the battle. A happier note is that in the nineteenth century in a meadow nearby called Leslie's Field, a quantity of silver plate was found. There is also supposed to be some gold, paid to the Earl of Traquair for betraying Montrose, thrown into a well or pond near Hangingshaw, but it has never been found.

Montrose's retreat to the Highlands (*Radio Times Hulton Picture Library*)

Preston I/17-18 August 1648

The defeat of Montrose at Philiphaugh was not the end of the Royalist cause in Scotland. In fact, there were many Royalists who were anti-Montrose because of his wild Highlanders, Irish and pro-Catholic troops, and they now joined the Duke of Hamilton, a moderate Presbyterian who had many friends in England but lacked Montrose's military genius. The Second Civil War broke out when Langdale seized Berwick and both Scarborough and Pontefract Castles declared for the Royalists. The most serious rising was in Wales and Cromwell went to deal with Pembroke Castle where Powell, an ex-Parliamentarian, had raised an army of 8,000 men. General Lambert was left to deal with the northern rising.

Hamilton's army of about 10,000 crossed the border on 8 July intending to make for Wales. They were joined by Langdale who had collected 3,000 foot and 600 horse, and a small army from Ireland under Sir George Monro. Unknown to the Royalists, who became very spread out due to having to find food and

Winwick church; in a defile nearby the Scots made their last stand against Cromwell (*author*)

shelter, Cromwell was on his way north to help Lambert. Pembroke Castle succumbed quickly to Cromwell's siege guns and the Welsh rising was over.

The Battle

On 16 August the Parliamentary army was in Stonyhurst Park near Preston; it only numbered about 8,500, but they were well armed and well led. Langdale spotted them and, to help the Scots infantry cross the Darwen to reach Wigan where the cavalry were quartered, he offered to hold his men as a rearguard and stop the Parliamentary forces from breaking into Preston. Hamilton led his horse back to help Langdale when the latter was in trouble. There was a very confused fight—Langdale holding his position for six hours and Hamilton's horse attempting to hold the bridge. Eventually Cromwell's horse got through some unguarded lanes and reached the bridge before Langdale. The latter extracted his horse and, with Hamilton, got over a ford to join the Scottish foot at Walton. Darkness came and the Scottish horse under Middleton, hurrying back from Wigan to help, passed the foot unseen on the way—presumably taking the road through Chorley while the foot was at Standish—and reached Walton to be met by Cromwell. Middleton turned back pursued by Thornhaugh's regiment which was routed by the Royalists and Thornhaugh killed. This was the only Royalist success.

In Langdale's words: 'I kept my post with varying success many times gathering ground of the enemy, and as the Scots Foot acknowledged they never saw any fight better than mine did: ... I having spent nine barrels of powder, the Scots continued their march over the river and did not secure a lane near the bridge, whereby some of the Parliamentary Forces came upon my flanks. Neither did the forces which were left for my supply come to my relief, but continued in the rear of mine, nor did they ever face the enemy but in bringing up the rear. When most of the Scots were drawn up over the

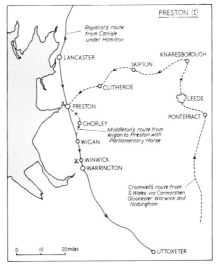

bridge, the Parliament Forces pressed hard upon me in the Van and Flanks, and so drive me into the Town, where the Duke (Hamilton) was with some horse, but all being lost, retreated over a ford to his foot.'

In the dark most of Langdale's horse escaped to the north where they joined up with Monro whose Royalists never reached Preston, and together they retreated back to Scotland where the force disbanded, Monro returning to Ulster. Most of Langdale's brave foot surrendered. The Scots foot, soaked and exhausted, turned at Winwick to face Cromwell. For three hours they held him back in a defile. Many fled to the church where they were rounded up and captured. Baillie and 2,600 Scottish infantry surrendered in Warrington and only Hamilton and a few cavalry escaped to Uttoxeter where they were captured. Hamilton was later executed in London; Langdale had better luck—he disguised himself as a Parliamentary soldier and escaped from Nottingham Castle making his way to Houghton Hall. Here he was surrounded by Fairfax's men but again escaped dressed as a milkmaid. Then he swam the Humber and made his way south to London in a clergyman's cloak; he hid in a friend's house there until making his way to the continent. His escape was almost as dramatic as that of Prince Charles after Worcester.

Preston Today

There is a dramatic picture of the bridge battle at the Harris Museum in Preston. The present church at Winwick is Victorian. There is a modern plaque on the Unicorn Cafe near Walton Bridge in Preston, but otherwise little to see today.

91

Dunbar/3 September 1650

Cromwell at Dunbar

The death of Montrose in 1649 coincided with a treaty made between the Scottish Estates and Charles II at Breda whereby Charles agreed to support the Covenant and Scottish Presbyterianism in exchange for the Scottish crown. Charles crossed to Scotland in 1650 and Argyll, destroyer of Montrose, set about levying a Scottish army. As its commander he had the victor of Newburn Ford, General Leslie, who was about to fight against his old Marston Moor allies, Cromwell and his captains. The Scottish army was hampered by preachers and the experienced commanders were replaced by those who 'believed in the miracles wrought by a pacified Jehovah'.

Cromwell crossed in July to Berwick with 11,000 foot and 5,000 horse, the pick of the New Model Army. Leslie managed to keep Cromwell at bay round Edinburgh without actually coming to grips with him and Cromwell was forced to fall back to Dunbar, his chief source of supply. After storming Redhall Tower, Cromwell was watched closely by Leslie, whose army was nearly 20,000 'minister's sons, clerks and such as who hardly ever saw or heard of

any sword but that of the spirit', camped in the rain on Doon Hill. With his headquarters at Broxburn House, Cromwell hoped that Leslie would descend the hill where he would have favourable ground as the steep sides of the Spott Burn would

Oliver Cromwell (*Radio Times Hulton Picture Library*)

92

make rapid movements difficult on Leslie's side. In front of Cromwell the Brox Burn was the line held during the night of 2 September by Cromwell who, having noticed Leslie's men descend from the hill, determined to attack with combined horse and foot early on the following day.

The Battle

Leslie's men suffered during the wet night and they extinguished their match used for lighting their muskets. In the early morning Cromwell's horse, commanded by Fleetwood, Whalley and Twisleton (Commander of Denbigh Castle) attacked, supported by two infantry regiments. The Scots were ready for them and held them; a regiment of Scottish lancers fought bravely and drove some of the Ironsides back. The foot of both sides were locked together at push of pike for nearly two hours. Many Highlanders perished and a regiment from Kirkness lost thirty officers including its Colonel, who was buried later near Broxburn House.

Leslie's hard-pressed right wing eventually collapsed and fell back on his centre. The second cavalry charge 'made by the Lord of Hosts as stubble to our swords' and the rout started; over 3,000 Scots were wounded or killed and many more captured. Leslie and most of the horse and some of the left wing got back to Stirling. Edinburgh fell to Cromwell and Heselrig, in command of the prisoners, was particularly brutal in marching them to Durham. They were so famished that many ate cabbages out of the fields and leaves from the hedges; others had to be killed by the guards because they were too weak to make the march. Some six hundred were locked in the cathedral and the same number in the castle. The fortunate ones, says James Grant, were the two hundred who were shipped to Virginia.

Dunbar Today

A modern monument stands beside the A1 beside a bus shelter and the Portland

The Dunbar memorial stone (*author*)

Cement Works. It is inscribed with the words of Thomas Carlyle 'Here took place the brunt or essential agony of the battle of Dunbar'. On the pedestal are the two watchwords of the armies: 'The Covenant' and 'The Lord of Hosts'.

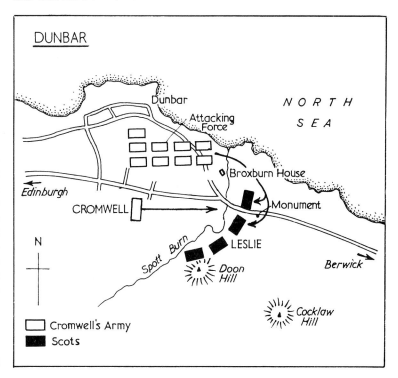

Worcester/3 September 1651

The remains of Leslie's army were defeated at Inverkeithing in April 1651 and Cromwell advanced as far as Perth. Charles II at Falkland had support from the Duke of Hamilton and the Duke of Buckingham; he had Leslie's reserves and also some of the Dunbar survivors, anxious to revenge the defeat. Avoiding both Edinburgh and Glasgow, Charles's army arrived at Carlisle on 6 August where Charles was proclaimed King. Like Bonny Prince Charlie 94 years later, few English recruits joined him and the populace were anxious to avoid involvement, the army being forced to pillage for its supplies which did

WORCESTER

LESLIE

R. Severn

WORCESTER

Leominster

Cathedral

Fort Royal

Hereford

Red Hill

Powick Bridge

Scots under HAMILTON

R. Teme

LAMBERT

Ketch Inn

Powick Malvern

FLEETWOOD

Kempsey

☐ Parliamentary Army
◪ Royalist/Scots Horse
■ Royalist Foot

1 Cromwell's 1st position
2 Cromwell's 2nd position
•• Boat bridges

not improve relations with the local people.

Cromwell was caught at Perth with a week's delay, but he sent Lambert and the cavalry to try to stop the Scots at Warrington. They were too late, but a force under Lambert with some Cheshire levies defeated the Earl of Derby, who had landed from the Isle of Man with some cavalry. The Scots arrived at Worcester, where Charles stopped to rest his troops and to give any hoped-for reinforcements from Wales a chance of appearing. Cromwell had by now reached Doncaster and, collecting men from Nottingham, he proceeded to Coventry,

Stratford and Evesham, cutting off Charles's route to London.

The Scots spent the week fortifying Worcester and Cromwell gathered boats from far and wide to make a bridge to cross the Severn and the Teme and unite his army, which was on both banks; because Leslie had destroyed all the bridges, one side could not help the other if it was attacked.

The Battle

Cromwell believed in superstition and, 3 September being the anniversary of Dunbar, he decided to attack. Lambert found that the bridge at Upton was only partly destroyed and managed to get his men across in spite of Scottish interference, which melted away when their leader, Massey, was wounded. Fleetwood in the meantime floated the bridge of boats down to the Teme–Severn junction where they were secured from bank to bank with, surprisingly, no opposition from the Scots. Fierce fighting took place at Powick Bridge, scene of the first skirmish in the Civil War. Gradually Fleetwood and Lambert pressed in on the western bank. Charles, watching from the cathedral tower, and seeing that the enemy on the eastern bank were leaderless and isolated after Cromwell had gone to consult Fleetwood, personally led a charge against them. For a time some of Cromwell's artillery was captured. Leslie would not use the Scottish horse in support however and the danger was soon seen by Cromwell who took some of his best troops back over the bridge of boats to help his right wing.

The gentlemen Royalists tried to force back the attacking Parliamentary infantry from the streets of Worcester and a last-ditch stand was made near the town hall. The young Duke of Hamilton was mortally wounded outside the Commandery and many others died in the narrow streets. Leslie led his horse out by the north gate, where it reached Cheshire before being overhauled by Lilburn's horse. The Earl of Derby was captured and later executed

The Commandery (*author*)

An old print showing (*top*) a view of Worcester with the battle raging on the meadows, (*centre*) the flight of Prince Charles, and (*bottom*) the wooden house where Charles lodged (*Radio Times Hulton Picture Library*)

and Charles, escorted by one or two faithful followers, slipped out of a house in New Street, reached Boscobel, and eventually, after some weeks of hide-and-seek, obtained a boat at Shoreham across the Channel. Cromwell called Worcester 'his crowning mercy'. Of the Royalist army of 13,000, barely 3,000 escaped; many were transported to America or sold as slaves. Leslie was imprisoned in the Tower and General Montgomery, who had gallantly defended Powick Bridge, in Edinburgh Castle. Supreme generalship and overwhelming numbers had won Worcester. With Dunbar it was probably Cromwell's finest victory and it ended the Civil War.

Worcester Today

The house where Charles escaped from still stands in New Street and the Commandery is a museum with a room devoted to the battle; in the cathedral is a monument to the Duke of Hamilton. If you stop at the Ketch Inn on the A44 you can see the spot 500 yards back along the river where the bridge of boats was constructed.

Sedgemoor/6 July 1685

Perhaps no other battle fought on British soil arouses quite so much fervour and discussion as Sedgemoor. Where was King James's army three years later when William of Orange landed? Why did Monmouth not succeed and why, if James was so unpopular in 1688, was he popular enough three years before for so many to take his side against Monmouth? Possibly the real reason was that Monmouth's claim to the throne was not strong enough: he was illegitimate as his mother's marriage to Charles II had never been finalised. The fact that he was a Protestant and James a Catholic was not a strong enough argument. When he landed in Lyme in June 1685, few people of note joined him; the old Puritans of the Westcountry who had cheered his progress a few years before gave him their support, especially the men from Taunton. His best assets were his charm and military knowledge—he had fought well at Bothwell Bridge—and his Dutch gunner and three cannon. Lord Grey who joined him and commanded his horse was not much

JAMES D. OF MONMOUTH.

The Duke of Monmouth
(*National Portrait Gallery*)

of a cavalry commander, but Wade, Holmes, Foulkes, Basset and Matthews were competent enough field commanders. Their men were poorly armed and many had taken scythes or billhooks normally used for cutting local withies for basket-making. Those who had muskets had barely enough rounds for more than a few shots.

Monmouth's route to Sedgemoor via Axminster, where he defeated some local militiamen, to Norton St Philip, where he drove back Lord Grafton's horse, was fairly successful. Realising he could not capture Bristol, he turned back and reached Bridgwater on 3 July, followed by Lord Feversham's Royalist army, without being able to get further east than Frome because the Wiltshire Militia were blocking one route and Feversham another.

On 5 July Feversham's army was at Westonzoyland. It was about 2,500 in number, 700 of which were dragoons and light horse, but it had no less than 17 guns. However, it consisted of the King's Horse Guards and Regiment of Horse and the Royal Dragoons, the 1st Guards, the 2nd Guards, Dumbarton's and Trelawney's and the fierce Colonel Kirke and his Tangier regiment, known as 'Kirke's Lambs'. (The modern names of these regiments in the same order are Life Guards, Royal Horse Guards (Regiment of Horse and Royal Dragoons), Grenadiers, Coldstreams, Royal Scots, King's Own and Queen's Royal Regiment.) They were well disciplined and Feversham, though slow, was not the incompetent commander that history often relates, though he did have the advantage of having John Churchill, future Duke of Marlborough, as his second-in-command. He sent out Sir Francis Compton to Chedzoy with some horse and Colonel Oglethorpe to Bawdip with his Horse Guards, the 'Blues', to act as scouts, and sat down to await events.

Monmouth knew that he must act soon or his army would disintegrate. He considered making a further move on Bristol but a Chedzoy farm servant named

Godfrey came to him offering to guide him over the moor to attack Feversham from the north west. It was a bold scheme and to make it even bolder Monmouth proposed to his council that it should be done at night. Taking the Bristol Road, Monmouth turned towards Bawdrip and crossed onto the moor at Peasey Farm. It was very dark and his men had been sworn to silence; the King's patrols in Chedzoy and Bawdrip slept soundly. Godfrey had trouble finding the ford across the Langmoor Rhine, a large drainage

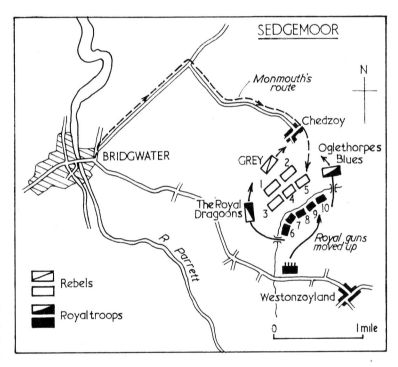

ditch, where the noise of a pistol shot alerted a sentry who warned Compton at Chedzoy. Monmouth pushed on slowly sending Grey's horse ahead to secure the bridge over the Bussex Rhine, the next ditch they had to find. In the meantime Compton's horse tried to get through to the same bridge from Chedzoy and ran into Grey. There was a confused fight and

1 Foulkes
2 Basset
3 Wade
4 Holmes and Monmouth
5 Matthews
6 2nd Guards
7 1st Guards
8 Dumbarton's
9 Kirke's
10 Trelawney's

The Sedgemoor monument
(*author*)

Compton was wounded, but not badly enough to prevent him successfully getting through to base and alerting Feversham.

The Battle

Monmouth still had the upper hand and his regiments were in position with the three Dutch guns in the middle soon firing at the Royalists on the other side of the Bussex Rhine before Feversham had realised quite what was happening. For a start the Royal guns were covering the Bridgwater road and had it not been for the Bishop of Winchester—who was present with the Royal army—lending the gunner his coach horses, the rebel guns would have done a lot more damage. What few musketeers Monmouth had were soon blazing away, but their carts of ammunition left at Peasey Farm were lost when Grey's horse, frustrated at the Upper Plungeon and fired on in the dark by some rebels, bolted and frightened off the cart drivers. Oglethorpe's horse appeared having discovered Bridgwater empty of rebels and were sent over the Upper Plungeon while the King's Royal Horse were despatched over the lower one. Oglethorpe was held up for some time by part of Grey's Horse under Captain Jones. Meanwhile Churchill brought up Trelawney's and Kirke's

regiments into the right of the line to assist Dumbarton's which was catching all the rebel fire and had lost most of its officers. The real reason for Monmouth losing was at the coming of daylight; his men deserted when their ammunition ran out—the carts had been taken away—and only the Mendip miners made a final stand, fighting to the last. Wade withdrew his regiment out of line of the musket fire and most of them surrendered. Monmouth and Lord Grey, who reappeared in the daylight, made off to the Polden Hills. Feversham's men all crossed the ditch and the battle was over.

Many wounded prisoners were locked up in the church at Westonzoyland and during the night two escaped, eventually getting across the Bristol Channel in a boat. They were the lucky ones. Rebels were hung at trees and gallows all over the Westcountry and Judge Jeffreys' Bloody Assizes are infamous.

Conclusion

Monmouth failed because he took a gamble that did not succeed; night marches are extremely difficult to carry out and to allow the ammunition cart drivers to ride off was a mistake. He was also opposed by some very efficient regiments. The fact that William succeeded three years later was partly due to the disloyalty of Churchill and to the fact that James was then well known to his army, who did not like him enough to want to fight for him. They had also seen what Jeffreys had done to the rebel survivors. It is true that the army could have made some resistance, but perhaps the real reason was that William and Mary had a legitimate claim to the throne, whereas Monmouth had not. Monmouth was dead; James saw him after he was captured. in a ditch near Ringwood, and refused him a pardon. Lord Grey was pardoned and lived for many years.

The Battlefield Today

The battlefield is a few miles out of Bridgwater on the A372. Turn off at Weston-

The capture of Monmouth
(*Radio Times Hulton Picture Library*)

zoyland (the church has a battle plan and list of rebels as well as a marvellous carved roof). Proceed down Monmouth Road to a farm and leave your car there. The monument is half-a-mile further on beneath two tall white willow trees and is worth the walk. The land has been so altered that the original Bussex Rhine no longer exists. There is a local Sedgemoor Society. Bridgwater's museum has a room devoted to the battle.

Killiecrankie/27 July 1689

The opposition to William of Orange in England was negligible, perhaps because the army of James II was so unpopular after its severe treatment of Monmouth's men at Sedgemoor. In Scotland, however, one of James's lieutenants was in command—Viscount Dundee who had served under Monmouth at Bothwell Bridge and was a natural leader. Supported by the

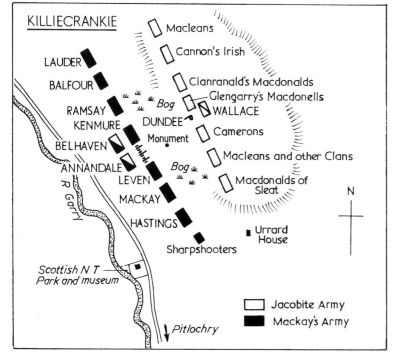

landers and drew up in position facing them. Presumably there were less trees then but they must have realised that neither cavalry nor their three small cannon would be of much use in such a steep valley. Dundee kept them waiting for two hours before giving the Macdonells and Macdonalds on his right and the Camerons and other clans on his left the signal to charge. Mackay's left instantly gave way and his right only had time to fire three rounds. The Earl of Dunfermline and sixteen horsemen captured the cannon and the English horse under Annandale and Belhaven was the first to flee. The English right under Mackay was steadier but when the latter tried to charge through with what was left of his cavalry, he found himself alone with one sergeant who had obeyed his command. The English had left some sharpshooters in Urrard House and one of these shot Dundee in the side; he was carried to the local inn where he died. His friend, Lord Pitcur, was also killed

local clans he made his base at Blair Atholl. The Scottish Convention sent General Mackay and about 5,000 regular troops to disperse the Highlanders. Dundee planned to catch Mackay's force, almost twice his in strength, at Killiecrankie Pass, where the Highlanders could fight on land of their chosing and not have to put up with English cavalry charges. The weather was fine and Dundee's men were arranged in position early on the hill overlooking the road Mackay would have to take to reach Blair Castle, whose owner was uncommitted to either side.

The Battle

The English army soon spotted the High-

The Soldier's Leap in the Pass of Killiecrankie; one of McKay's men escaped by jumping over this torrent (*The National Trust for Scotland*)

and the two were buried at Blair Atholl. Mackay retreated with 400 survivors to Stirling, leaving his baggage, 500 prisoners and about 1,500 dead on the field, amongst them Lord Balfour who was killed by the Rev Robert Stewart, a volunteer in Dundee's army who wielded a sword with terrible effect. The English baggage was the main attraction for the Scottish troops and its plundering saved a lot of lives for Mackay.

Aftermath

Killiecrankie was an isolated event and Colonel Cannon, who led Dundee's Irish in the battle, took over command, but had not the power to control the Highlanders. They attacked Dunkeld where Mackay's Cameronian regiment were firmly entrenched and after a short but bloody struggle killed Cleland, the Cameronian leader, and set half the village on fire although failing to capture it. Cannon retired to Mull and the rebellion collapsed.

The Battlefield Today

Well supplied with a car park, souvenir stall and taped commentary of the battle, the National Trust of Scotland has organised Killiecrankie extremely well. However, the discerning tourist will be surprised to know that the above facilities are not on the battlefield. The latter, privately owned, is on the other side of the road and has a memorial on it to the memory of Ian Campbell the Younger of Urrard, who was killed in Malaya aged 24 in 1950. It is a peaceful scene, heather, trees and bog covering the hillside where Dundee made his final charge.

Viscount Dundee (*Radio Times Hulton Picture Library*)

101

The Boyne/1 July 1690

Although situated in County Meath, southern Ireland, The Boyne is essentially a British battle. It was this victory, along with Killicrankie, that established William on the throne; had James won, the Jacobite battle might not have taken place.

An engraving of the battle with troops crossing the ford in the centre (*Bord Failte*)

The 'bloodless revolution' of 1688 and James II's hurried departure for France did not end the struggle. Scotland was in arms and Dundee's death had not altered the animosity of Scottish Catholics towards English and Dutch Protestants. In Ireland the Lord Deputy, Tyrconnell, collected a large army of Stuart supporters and when James landed with French arms, money and 3,000 men at Kinsale, he was joined by Tyrconnell and his army. The siege of Londonderry and the strong resistance of the Protestant population was heartening for William, who was distrustful of the English army that had deserted James, preferring his Dutch regulars. He sent a large army of 16,000 under the command of eighty-four-year-old Marshal Schomberg to Carrickfergus. Two battalions of Dutch guards and some Huguenot regiments were in the Williamite army as well as dragoons from Scotland and some new regiments, the descent of which can be traced to existing foot regiments today. The following year the King arrived in person with more troops, including some Danes under the Duke of Wirtemberg, and accompanying the King were Prince George of Denmark, the Duke of Ormonde and the Earl of Oxford.

James decided to retreat to Dublin when William landed in the north in June, and his Irish advisers suggested defending a position on the Boyne, so battle was inevitable. His cavalry commanded by the Duke of Berwick and Richard Hamilton, and the French troops under Lauzun, were his strongest arm, but his army of about 30,000 was outnumbered by William's army of 36,000. The stage was set for the struggle that was not only going to decide the future of Ireland, but of England too. The opening Jacobite cannon fire was effective. The Prince of Hesse's horse was killed and a six-pounder grazed William who was mounting his horse next to the Prince. In Paris they received news that Dutch William had been killed and the Bastille guns fired to celebrate a victory. The truth was the reverse.

The Battle

William's objective was to get his army

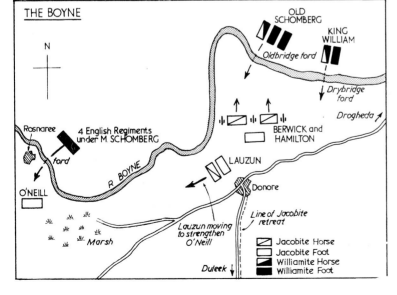

THE BOYNE

N

OLD SCHOMBERG

KING WILLIAM

Oldbridge ford

Drybridge ford

Drogheda

BERWICK and HAMILTON

Rosnaree

4 English Regiments under M. SCHOMBERG

ford

R. BOYNE

O'NEILL

LAUZUN

Donore

Line of Jacobite retreat

Lauzun moving to strengthen O'Neill

Marsh

Duleek

	Jacobite Horse
	Jacobite Foot
	Williamite Horse
	Williamite Foot

across the river. He had fords at Rosnaree, Oldbridge and Drybridge and he split his army into three, his own group taking Drybridge, Old Schomberg the centre ford and his son, Meinhart, the right ford a mile away at Rosnaree. Tyrconnell's Irish infantry had thrown up fortifications opposite Oldbridge and Drybridge fords and O'Neill and his dragoons protected the other ford. Lauzun and the French regiments now dashed off to help the hard-pressed O'Neill, thus weakening the defences of Drybridge and Oldbridge fords. At 10.15 in the morning Schomburg's infantry waded armdeep over the Boyne. La Caillemote, commander of one of the French Huguenot regiments, was killed by the Jacobite guns, which were all directed onto the river. Hamilton led his horse against the French who had got across and King James's regiment of horse held off the Huguenots, who were now leaderless. Old Marshal Schomberg himself tried to rally them but was cut down and killed by the cavalry. Berwick and Hamilton led no less than ten charges to try to force the Protestants back over the river. The Irish infantry fled in disorder. Many confused friend with foe and even King William had to stop one of his own soldiers from shooting a pistol at him. 'What, are you angry with your friends?' he is supposed to have said, making the man and his regiment into his bodyguard.

Lauzun had been unable to stop the four English regiments crossing at Rosnaree as the boggy land hindered his horses. However he was able to supervise the retreat with Berwick, as Hamilton had been captured. James, realising that William's horse was at Donore, and that if he was cut off at Duleek he might not extract his army, ordered the retreat. Lauzun's French regiments formed an effective rearguard and for seven miles the pursuit followed. The unfortunate James took to a ship for Brest and his army lost all its baggage, arms and ammunition. It suffered some 1,500 casualties and William's about 500. The war carried on for another year. There was a further

battle at Aughrim and when Sarsfield surrendered Limerick, the Williamite party had won the day. The Boyne is celebrated to this day as the greatest victory of Irish Protestant over Irish Catholic, a struggle that seems to be with us for a long time to come.

The Boyne Today

The crossing where the Dutch guards and Huguenots fought the Irish is in the park of a big house. Donore is a few cottages with a ruined church half-a-mile away to the south. Oldbridge hamlet has vanished but there is still King William's Glen.

Old Schomberg—William's commander killed in the battle (*National Army Museum*)

103

Preston II/13 November 1715

The execution of Lords Derwentwater and Kenmure on Tower Hill, February 1716

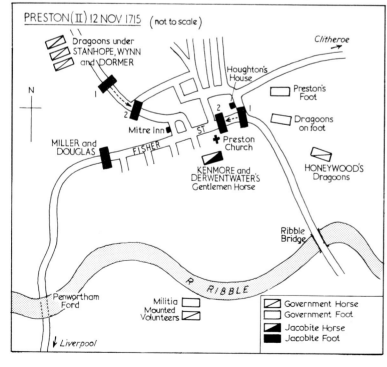

The '15 Rising was as remarkable in many ways as The '45. In England it had more support than its more illustrious successor, support that was perhaps more idealistic than militarily useful. The Earl of Derwentwater and 'General' Forster with a party of volunteer gentlemen horse —'fox hunters with light dress-swords' they have been called—met up in Kelso with Viscount Nithsdale, Lords Kenmure Wintoun and Carnwath and Brigadier Mackintosh's 2,000 Highlanders, who were the backbone of their small army. A dispute as to where to go next nearly finished the party but eventually Macintosh was persuaded to march south for Penrith. Forster, who held his commission from Mar, had great hopes of obtaining help from the Lancashire Catholics.

Few came to their support, however, and there were always Scottish deserters to equal the numbers of the new recruits. On 9 November the horse reached Preston. The following day Mackintosh's foot arrived with some of the Atholl regiment under Lord Charles Murray. General Wills was on his way from Cheshire with dragoons and Preston's foot regiment to deal with the invasion and General Carpenter was on his way from Newcastle to help. On 11 November Murray, Mackintosh and some of the soldiers realised that they were undefended. Forster was not prepared to block the Ribble bridge, so four barricades were hastily made in the town. Some naval cannon strengthened Mackintosh of Borlum's barricade by the church. Captains

104

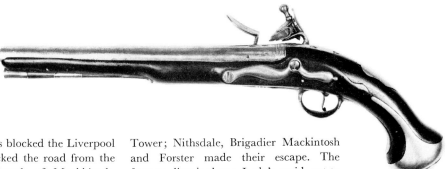

Miller and Douglas blocked the Liverpool road, Murray blocked the road from the north and Mackintosh of Mackintosh, second in command of the clan, blocked the road from Blackpool.

The Battle

The approaching Wills was surprised to see that no Jacobite force defended the bridge. He allowed his men across slowly and his first attack on Mackintosh's position near the church was repulsed with at least 120 casualties amongst Wills's dismounted dragoons and Preston's foot. Wills suffered similar setbacks at the two other barricades. Only Miller and Douglas seemed to have no action, apart from letting deserters escape through their barricade. The night saw a certain amount of sniping; some of the English forces got into Houghton's house and enfiladed Mackintosh's barrier, forcing him to retire to a further one. There was much arguing between the English and Scots, and next morning Carpenter arrived. He did not take over the command from Wills but made several suggestions, including the sending of fresh troops to block Fisher Street, where Miller and Douglas's barricade was positioned.

The Surrender

The Scots were unaware at first that Forster had sent Oxburgh out to obtain surrender terms. The Scots reluctantly agreed to a surrender. Of the Jacobites, 17 were killed and 25 wounded; over two hundred Government troops had been killed and wounded. One of them, Colonel Preston of Preston's foot, was struck down at Murray's barricade. Nicholas Wogan, a Jacobite volunteer, climbed the barricade and rescued the Colonel, thus securing his pardon. Others were not so lucky: the leaders were condemned to the

Tower; Nithsdale, Brigadier Mackintosh and Forster made their escape. The former, disguised as a Lady's maid, got to France and the other two escaped from Newgate but both Derwentwater and Viscount Kenmure were executed. The rank and file were locked in Preston church for a month. Many were transported overseas and some eventually made their way home to Scotland. A few fought in The '45, including Nicholas Wogan who also fought at Fontenoy.

Preston Today

There are few relics of The '15 at Preston today. In the Harris Museum in the Market Square are a couple of swords and there are other relics of the 1648 battle. The Earl of Derwentwater's home, Langley Castle, Northumberland, is open to the public. Strangely enough it was built by Sir Thomas Lucy, who saved the day at Neville's Cross (*see* p 26).

The Old Pretender—Prince James Francis Edward Stuart (*National Portrait Gallery*)

Sheriffmuir/13 November 1715

Government Army (Argyll)

Front Line:
1 Carpenter's dragoons
2 Kerr's dragoons
3 & 4 Stair's dragoons
5 6 battalions (1,800 men)
   under General Wightman
6 Stair's dragoons
7 Scots Greys
8 Evans's dragoons
9 60 volunteer gentlemen

Second Line:
10 2 battalions of infantry
11 & 12 Dragoons

Jacobite Army (Mar)

Front Line:
13 & 14 Huntly's horse
15 Stirling horse
16 General Gordon's
   Highlanders (10 battalions)
17 Perth horse
18 Fife horse

Second Line:
19 Earl Marischal's horse
   (2 battalions)
20–22 Seaforth's Highlanders
   (3 battalions)
23 & 24 Huntly's Highlanders
   (2 battalions)
25 Panmure
26 Tullibardine
27 Drummond
28 Strathallan
29 Robertsons
30 Angus horse
31 Reserve (800 men)

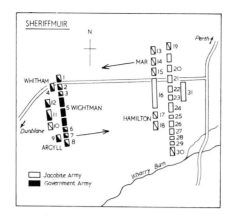

The Jacobite Rebellion of 1715 was in many respects more promising initially than the 1745. At first there was more French support in spite of the fact that Louis XIV had died the month before the Earl of Mar, George I's recently dismissed Secretary of State for Scotland, raised his standard at Braemar. Even with a commission from James VIII in his hand, many clan chiefs were still not particularly keen on the Earl as a leader, but the Hanoverian government insisted that they should go to Edinburgh and pay bail for their loyalty which drove them to rebellion. The Earl gathered his army at Perth, moving slowly to Auch-

terarder where Gordon, with his Fife and Huntly's horse and his Highlanders, joined him. Mar, anxiously awaiting a move from the Duke of Ormonde on the continent who was supposed to be invading the west of England, did not hurry. His plan was to approach the Forth in four divisions and, as his army was 10,000 strong by November, he was not afraid of the opposition under Argyll and Wightman at Stirling which, according to his scouts, consisted of a mere 3,000 men.

General Gordon's contingent was ordered forward by Mar to occupy Dunblane but, advised of this, Argyll got there first and camped nearby above Kippenross House on the edge of Sheriffmuir, country he knew well as it was the training ground of the Menteith Militia. General Gordon fell back to Kinbuck and the next morning, 13 November, Mar joined him and drew up his forces in two lines across the eastern end of Sheriffmuir. In the front line of the Jacobite army were Gordon's Highlanders, flanked on the right by Huntly's and the Stirling horse and on the left by Hamilton and his Perth and Fife horse. The second line was protected on the right flank by the Earl Marischal's horse and by the Angus horse (gentlemen riders) on the left, where there was a

The Earl of Mar's council of war (*Radio Times Hulton Picture Library*)

large bog. The centre consisted of ten infantry battalions. In the reserve was a further 800 men. Argyll positioned himself where the Gathering Stone stands and arranged his army, superior in cannon and cavalry but not in numbers, with his dragoon regiments on the left (Carpenter's, Kerr's and Stair's), General Wightman's infantry in the centre and his own horse on the right. In reserve he had more dragoons and two battalions of infantry.

The Battle

The battle that followed was unusual by any standards and due to incompetent generalship on both sides neither wing of either army knew what the other wing was up to. The Highlanders on the right of Mar's army, chiefly McLeans, charged the horse and foot of General Whitham and chased them into the outskirts of Stirling. Many were killed and captured and four colours and fourteen hundred arms were captured. Meanwhile Argyll's right wing under Colonel Cathcart charged Hamilton's wing before it had finished getting into position and only the bravery of the Fife Horse stopped a complete rout. Many Highland leaders were captured, four of Mar's cannon taken and the Macraes in Seaforth's battalion were slaughtered almost to a man.

When Argyll returned to the battlefield after following up Cathcart's success he found his troops greatly outnumbered, for some of the Jacobite horse had remained behind rather than break their ranks in following Mar's right wing. The Jacobites could have attacked again and won a complete victory but orders were not forthcoming. As the Master of Sinclair said later 'the spirits of the best men on earth must be broken by such leaders'. Mar, when he returned, led his army off the field back to Perth, where most of it disbanded before the arrival of James VIII from France. The news from Preston when it came did not encourage any further action and the Rising petered out. Nearly 800 Jacobites were killed or captured to about 300 of Argyll's men.

There is supposed to have been a traitor in Mar's retinue at Sheriffmuir called Drummond who was taking a message from Mar to Hamilton, who could not see what was happening on the right; instead of telling him to attack he told him the right had been defeated and he should give way.

The Battlefield Today

Sheriffmuir is an unspoilt moor today easily reached from Stirling by a minor road. The large monument to the Macraes is near the road and behind it in the heather is the Gathering Stone, protected by iron hoops, where Argyll is supposed to have stood before the battle. In the Clan Donnachie Museum near Blair Atholl can be seen the Robertson's crystal stone, the *Clach na Brattich*, which was carried at both Sheriffmuir and Culloden.

Glen Shiel/10 June 1719

The type of grenade used by **General Wightman** (*National Army Museum*)

An impression of the battle

The high cost of the 1715 Rising was partly met by the pension paid by the French government to Mary of Modena. On her death in May 1718, the Jacobites on the continent turned for support to Cardinal Alberoni in Spain. Prompted by the Duke of Ormonde, he raised a fleet and a small armada for invasion of England. The Earl Marischal, one of the leaders at Sheriffmuir, and his brother James Keith, future Prussian field marshal, were the main leaders of the 1719 affair, which was the smallest of the risings and in some ways the most unusual. England was at war with Spain and Byng had destroyed the Spanish Mediterranean fleet at Cape Passaro in 1718, but Alberoni still had a fleet at Cadiz. In early March 1719 it set off for England with 5,000 troops and arms for six times that number. Shortly after this a second expedition of only two ships, 300 Spanish troops, arms for 2,000, money and ammunition set out for Scotland with the two Keiths, while in another ship from France the Marquis of Tullibardine, appointed leader by James of the expedition, arrived at Lewis in April with the Earl of Seaforth who, having plotted with the Swedish court for a Swedish army to support the invasion, was also considered a leader. Meanwhile the Keiths had not realised that the Ormonde's fleet had been scattered by storm—like its more famous

predecessor in 1588. They had given notice to the western clans not to come out until they received news of Ormonde's landing. There was argument about the leadership when Tullibardine and Seaforth arrived but eventually the former won and set up an arsenal at Eilean Donan Castle in Loch Duich. He was foiled by the Royal Navy, for the frigates *Worcester*, *Enterprize* and *Flamborough* arrived and blew up the arsenal with cannon fire.

The Battle

General Wightman, who had fought well at Sheriffmuir and was now in command at Inverness, had about 1,100 men, including a Dutch regiment, Montagu's infantry, a few dragoons and four light Coehorn mortars. He quickly set out for Glen Shiel. The Marquis of Tullibardine now tried to gather the clans, but it was too late to get more than a few Mackenzies, Macraes and Macgregors. However Lord George Murray came with his men from

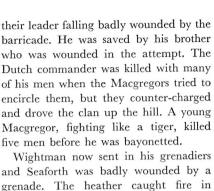

their leader falling badly wounded by the barricade. He was saved by his brother who was wounded in the attempt. The Dutch commander was killed with many of his men when the Macgregors tried to encircle them, but they counter-charged and drove the clan up the hill. A young Macgregor, fighting like a tiger, killed five men before he was bayonetted.

Wightman now sent in his grenadiers and Seaforth was badly wounded by a grenade. The heather caught fire in places and the smoke, as much as the enemy, drove the Jacobites up the mountain. The pass was Wightman's for the loss of 142 men. The Spaniards all surrendered the following day and were marched to Edinburgh, but Tullibardine, Seaforth and Keith escaped abroad.

Glen Shiel Today

The site of the battle is about half a mile east of the new bridge and the grave of one of Montagu's officers is visible near a waterfall. Bullets are sometimes found in the riverbed and there is reputed to be Spanish treasure buried nearby. Eilean Donan Castle, blown up by the *Worcester*, was repaired by Colonel Macrae-Gilstrap in the 1920s and is open to the public.

Glen Shiel (*The National Trust for Scotland*)

1
2 } Grenadiers
3
4 Montagu
5 Harrison
6 Huffel's Dutch
7 Robertson's dragoons and 4 Coehorn mortars
8 Clayton's under Colonel Reading
9 Monro Highlanders
10 Sutherland

Atholl. Never had a Scottish army had so many leaders and so few men—it was Sheriffmuir in reverse. The track to Loch Duich passes over a bridge over the Shiel at the eastern end of the Loch. Here Tullibardine arranged his army: the Spaniards manned the barricade over the road, Murray crossed the river and placed his men on the far side with Seaforth and the Keiths manning the slopes of the massive Sgurr na Ciste Duibhe, which looms 3,370 feet above the narrow pass.

Early next morning, 10 June, the Mackenzie pipes played 'Tulloch Aird' and the yellow-coated Dutch and red-coated English came into position. Wightman hesitated about giving battle to the Jacobites in such a formidable defensive position but he had a numerical superiority and had his mortars—which terrified the Highlanders in the mountains—as well as his grenadiers. His Scottish troops, the Monroes, charged forward but were repulsed by the Mackenzies and Spaniards,

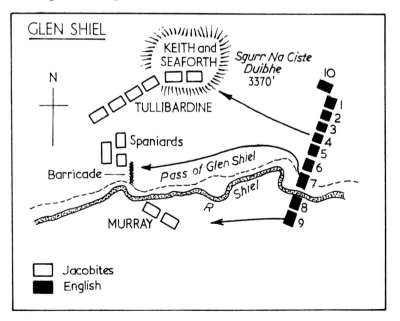

GLEN SHIEL

N

KEITH and SEAFORTH
Sgurr Na Ciste Duibhe 3370'

TULLIBARDINE

Spaniards

Barricade

Pass of Glen Shiel

R Shiel

MURRAY

□ Jacobites
■ English

10
1
2
3
4
5
6
7
8
9

The Jacobite Rebellion/1745-46

'The Gentle Lochiel'—a painting in the possession of Sir Donald Cameron of Lochiel (*Anthony MacMillan*)

Few events in British history are as well known as the Jacobite Rebellion. The Fifteen Rising was a slow sluggish affair with some half-hearted fighting and no decisive victory by either side. Perth was captured, the Old Pretender arrived too late and the Scottish Jacobite army melted away. In 1719 the little Spanish force was defeated by General Wightman and his new Coehorn mortars. However there was one person the Jacobites were prepared to rally round. Prince Charles Edward was twenty-four. He was a skilled swordsman, active, fit and, in spite of having a Polish mother and an accent that must have made him difficult to understand in Scotland, he was a born adventurer and had that rare quality of leadership that made men prepared to die for his cause. Ironically his father, who lived to 1766, would have become King

sons and remained at home themselves while a few took no part at all. From a military point of view, the first point to consider is the two armies.

The Jacobite Army

The clansmen were traditional fighters. They were armed with broadswords (not claymores—a claymore is a two-handed sword) which they sharpened themselves, and targes—round shields of wood and metal-studded leather which were held on the left arm for sword fighting but would not stop a bullet. They carried dirks in their stockings and some were armed with the Lochaber axe (one can be seen in the White Tower Collection in the Tower of London) which had a long handle, curved blade and a useful hook for pulling a man off a horse. Horsemen carried pistols and some of the clansmen carried them, but in general the Highlanders had little faith in firearms and would throw away their guns after using them once to close with their trusty swords. The artillery was of little significance and always an embarrassment to the Highlanders. There were some 30 pieces of ordnance at Culloden, mostly from French ships, and some 9-pounders captured from the English army. The foreign regiments —the Irish and French—were armed with firelocks, the flintlock musket which was rare, and the more common barrel-loading musket which was cumbersome. The Scots also had some ship's swivel guns.

A 'Clan' Regiment

Some confusion often occurs in reading histories of Scottish warfare because the clan system is not unstructured as might be thought, but organised on near-regimental lines. *The Camérons* (see Bibliography) lists the officers who were 'out' in The '45 for the clan (see Appendix, p 124).

The rank and file clansmen of the first line were tenants of the clan chief, Donald Cameron of Lochiel. They paid very little rent and this was reduced in return for military service when required. The

Typical uniforms of the Hanoverian army troops

had Charles succeeded, but the Jacobites were fighting for more than a King. They hated the Protestant Hanoverian rule; some of them hated the Union; some hated the Campbells—Glencoe had to be avenged—and it had been Argyll, a Campbell, who had thwarted their hopes at Sheriffmuir. The clan leaders, once convinced of the cause, were able to bring out their clans. Some sent their younger

heads of the cadet branches, Callart, Lundavra, Dungallon, and Erracht also had their 'kindly' tenants as they were called. Arms were supplied by the chief, though many had their own. Some 'kindly' tenants had special concessions as piper, armourer or bard. The second line troops, the ordinary clansmen, who paid rent in kind and usually worked on the land, were not so well armed. Many had to be forced to fight and some disappeared home with 'booty' after the battles. Some MacLeans fought with the Camerons and there was also a contingent of Mac-Millans from Locharkaig who had their own officers.

Some idea of how the clan system suffered after Culloden can be gathered from the Cameron casualties listed in the Appendix (p 124).

As with many Scottish clans, the later generations of Camerons took naturally to the army as a career. Two famous regiments—the 26th Cameronians and the 79th Queen's Own Cameron Highlanders —were formed from members of the clan; however, neither regiment exists in that name today, the Highlanders being amalgamated with the Seaforths in 1961. A stirring account of the 2nd Queen's Own Cameron Highlanders action at Keren Pass in World War II has recently been written by printer Peter Cochrane (*Charlie Company*, London 1977).

The Hanoverian Army

Cumberland's army had just seen action against the French at Fontenoy. His infantry were armed with the flintlock musket and bayonet, not the plug bayonet that had caused such problems at Killie-crankie, and were taught to fire in ranks. Loading was a complicated procedure; some powder was poured into the firing pan, some down the barrel followed by a paper wad and cartridge, and then the musket ball. The trigger when pulled, sparked the powder with a flint striker and the flame was supposed to go through the touch-hole and explode the cartridge. Accuracy was poor and the effective range

was a mere hundred yards. Non-commissioned officers had the spontoon, a pointed halberd which was really used for dress or sentry duties rather than a fighting weapon. Officers had pistols and swords, very often backswords (ie with one cutting edge unlike the broadsword which had two), while the infantryman's hanger was a joke, used more for camp cooking than fighting. The dragoons were overloaded with equipment. They were large men with infantry muskets, broad belts, cavalry swords, pistols usually worn on a chest strap and an ammunition pouch. They had large horses, like coach horses, and were very slow compared with their seventeenth-century predecessors. The Scottish horse had poorer horses but usually less equipment, so moved a bit faster. Cumberland's best arm was his

The Raising of the Standard in The '45 (*The National Trust for Scotland*)

artillery which, though stuck in the mud and abandoned at Falkirk, came into its own at Culloden. The 9-pound smooth-bore field guns were effective up to 700 yards with solid shot and could also fire grape or canister shot with devastating effect. Unlike the Scottish guns, most of Cumberland's were of the same bore and there was always enough ammunition.

111

Prestonpans/21 September 1745

Prestonpans monument (*author*)

The control of sea power was a vital part of The '45. Admiral Vernon's fleet was active and at the start HMS *Lion*, a man-of-war, encountered the *Elizabeth* which had 700 men and equipment on board for Charles's army. The latter was so badly damaged that it had to turn back to Brest. Charles's little ship, the *Du Teillay*, continued alone and in July landed him safely at Eriskay with his seven supporters. At first only the Macdonalds joined the Prince but after Cameron of Lochiel—known as 'Gentle Lochiel'—joined with his clan, the others came in. There had been a private agreement that none of them would join if Lochiel refused. At the Glenfinnan muster 700 Camerons, Macdonalds and Stewarts arrived, mostly without arms, and later Macdonald of Keppoch arrived with 300 of his clan and a few McLeods, for the Chief of the McLeods had refused to support so wild a scheme. In fact he wrote to the Scottish Lord President, Duncan Forbes, another Hanoverian supporter, saying that 'Not one man of any consequence beneath the Grampians will give any sort of assistance to this mad rebellious attempt'.

In the meantime at Stirling a new general had arrived to command the three infantry regiments, some 'loyal' Scots companies and Gardiner's and Hamilton's dragoons. This was General John Cope, an inexperienced soldier who 'was fitter for anything than the chief command in war'. Cope made for Inverness, frightened of being caught in an ambush and short of food, whence he took ship for Leith. Meanwhile Charles entered Perth, his army growing day by day. Here Lord George Murray joined Charles. Twice the Prince's age, he was by far the most competent general on either side during The '45, with the exception of a young officer on Hawley's staff, James Wolfe, but his day was still to come. When Cope landed at Dunbar on 17 September, having failed to get to Leith because of contrary winds, Charles was already in Edinburgh, where only the castle held out for the Hanoverians. On 20 September Charles's

army, now 2,400 men and a few horse, left Duddingston for Preston determined to attack Cope, whose army was smaller but much better equipped and trained although in a foreign country. Murray led the Jacobites to Falside Hill (*see* Pinkie Cleugh p 56). Guided by the son of a local laird, Anderson, the Highlanders descended the hill at 4.0 a.m. and lined up near Seton facing Cope's army at Prestonpans. To have fought them from the hill as Dundee might have done would have necessitated crossing a large morass. A dragoon on lookout duty heard them coming and at once woke Cope. The Hanoverian army had to deploy to the

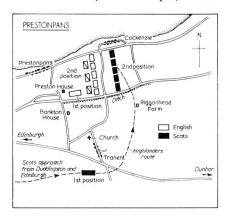

The Young Pretender, Prince Charles Edward

east, and the seaman gunners ran off with the artillery horses, so the guns remained on the right wing where they did very little damage. Charles arranged his men with the Camerons on the left and the Macdonalds on the right. In the rear were his gentlemen riders and in the second line were the men from Atholl. the Robertsons and the Maclachans.

The Battle

The speed of the Prestonpans victory was one of the astounding achievements of the Jacobite campaign. In the second line the Chevalier Johnstone, Murray's aide-de-camp, said 'we saw no other enemy on the field of battle than those who were lying on the ground killed and wounded'. The dragoons rode off as the first wave of Highlanders came in. The artillery fired one round, the mortars one round and Colonel Gardiner, who had played an important part in the 1715 Battle of Preston (*see* p 104) was shot twice and then cut down by a Highlander with a Lochaber axe when he fell off his horse. Cope attempted in vain to rally his dragoons and escaped with about 400 of them down a lane to the back of Preston House, known as Johnnie Cope's Road, eventually reaching Berwick-on-Tweed.

The Camerons led the charge and the Macdonalds on the right were not slow in following. Very few were killed, for the sun shone in the eyes of the Hanoverian infantry and Murray estimated that 40 were killed in the charge and about the same number wounded. Some 300 Hanoverians were killed and more wounded, and at least 1,600 prisoners were taken of which 70 were officers.

The entire baggage train was captured with a large sum of money. Of more use were the horses, though many were killed by Highland scythes and the cannon. Two important results of Prestonpans were that it persuaded the Prince that his army was invincible and it brought out more Highlanders in support. Two not so good results were that it made George II's ministers rush more troops over from the continent—Fontenoy had been fought and lost in May so they were not in the best of spirits but numbers were all on the Government side—and that the new generals, Hawley and the Duke of Cumberland were, unlike Cope, men of experience and while perhaps not of brilliance, certainly of competence.

Prestonpans Today

The battlefield is just off the A1 near Tranent. Beside a railway bridge is the monument. Preston House, where many of the wounded were taken after the battle, still stands impressively by the A198.

Clifton Moor/18 December 1745

Muskets dating from 1742
(*National Army Museum*)

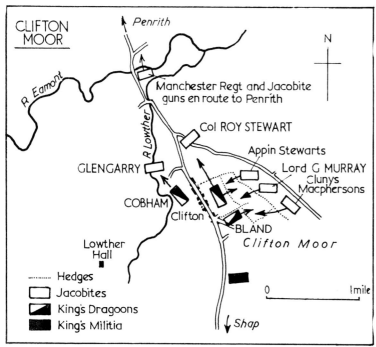

The Jacobite army reached Derby by 5 December, but the English and Welsh Jacobites were unenthusiastic. Apart from a few recruits in Manchester, there was no support. The Duke of Cumberland with 7,000 men blocked the road at Lichfield and General Wade at Newcastle could make a pass at Carlisle and cut off their retreat. News came from Scotland of the landing of the Duke of Perth with the Irish picquets and his own regiment—some 4,000 well armed trained men; Lord Strathallan, Jacobite commander in Scotland during the Prince's absence, had collected further recruits. The decision to retreat was a difficult one as it effected the morale of the army and of the Prince, but tactically it was sensible. Bad weather and broken bridges—the militia acted as a sort of guerilla force—slowed down the retreat and by 17 December the artillery and its escort of 500 Macdonalds was a day's march behind the rest of the army. A small force of militia got between the main army at Penrith and the rearguard under Murray at Clifton. There was a brief action and the Scots captured two men, one of whom was the Duke of Cumberland's footman. The Duke was following

up with 4,000 men, mostly dragoons. Reinforcements were sent for and Colonel Roy Stewart, Cluny Macpherson and the Stewart of Appin regiments came to reinforce Murray, who placed them in the hedges and behind the walls of Clifton, where the darkness concealed them from the approaching dragoons.

The Battle

Clifton battle was really a skirmish. The dragoons only had time to fire once before the Macphersons, Stewarts and Murray's men were on them. Fourteen swords were broken on the metal skull caps of the Englishmen, mostly Bland's dragoons. 'We did very well', said one Highlander after the fight, 'until the lang man in muckle boots came o'er the dyke'. This was Colonel Honeywood who commanded Bland's regiment; he was wounded and lost his sword. On the other flank the Glengarry regiment fired on the advancing Cobham's dragoons, whose white belts made them easy targets, and drove them back. The Stewarts formed the rearguard and the darkness soon ended the fight. Twelve men from Cluny's regiment who pursued too far were

captured. A few of these were executed in York and the others sent to America; one of the latter returned as a sergeant in the Royal Scots Regiment in France.

The Clifton skirmish was a triumph for Lord George Murray who fought so hard himself that he lost his wig and hat, and for Colonel Kerr who had brought up the reinforcements from Penrith. The Duke of Perth had sent the Atholl regiment to Lowther bridge as a further reinforcement but they took no part in the fight. By 19 December the whole army was safely at Carlisle and the Duke of Cumberland remained on Clifton Moor.

Clifton Today

On the main A6, Clifton is a tiny village six miles south of Penrith. There is a recent monument in the churchyard to the fallen of Bland's regiment erected by their successors—the Queen's Own Hussars. The area was very enclosed even then and it is difficult to be sure exactly where the battle took place, but an earthwork not far from the church was probably defended by Cluny's men.

The monument to Bland's regiment recently erected in Clifton churchyard (*author*)

Falkirk/17 January 1746

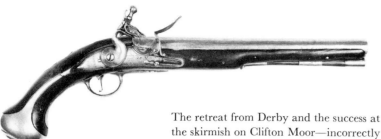

A 1728 pistol, the type used in The '45 (*National Army Museum*)

The retreat from Derby and the success at the skirmish on Clifton Moor—incorrectly called Clifton Muir in some accounts of The '45 written by Scots and the last battle on English soil—did not finish the run of Jacobite successes. Their army, re-equipped with shoes and funds by a reluctant Glasgow corporation, divided in two. Charles took one section to Bannock-burn and Lord George Murray the other to Falkirk. Lord John Drummond and the new recruits plus a few French soldiers like the Fitzjames horse—some of whom had had their horses captured at sea in a French transport ship—joined Charles in Stirling, where the town quickly sur-rendered to the Jacobites. The castle, however, under General Blakeney, held out for the Hanoverians and no amount of siege artillery could force its surrender; it was a perpetual thorn in the flesh of Charles and his army. Meanwhile General Hawley with an army of 8,000 men arrived in Edinburgh. Hawley had no respect for the Highlanders although he had fought at Sheriffmuir as well as Dettingen and Fontenoy, so he knew how they could fight. He imagined that well

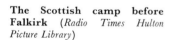

The Scottish camp before Falkirk (*Radio Times Hulton Picture Library*)

drilled cavalry could cut through them easily. Lord George Murray took advant-age of his knowledge of the Falkirk area to position the Highlanders on the hill overlooking the town south of the Stirling–Falkirk road. Lord John Drummond's men took a different route from Murray from Bannockburn to Falkirk and misled the spies in Hawley's army, which was encamped near Falkirk, who reported that an attack was a false alarm. At two o'clock on 17 January, however, another alarm was sent to Hawley's camp but the General was dining with the Countess of Kilmarnock at nearby Callander House and did not take the field until late in the day. He sent his dragoons up Maggie Wood's Loan to command the hill but the Highlanders were already in position. The infantry followed in a driving gale.

Lord George was careful in arranging the battle order. From left to right in the front rank he had Lochiel's Camerons, then the Stewarts, Frasers, Macintoshes, Farquharsons, Mackenzies and, on the right wing, the Macdonalds of Glencarry, Clanranald and Keppoch. Lord John Drummond with Lord Lewis Gordon's men, and the Ogilvy and Atholl regiments formed the second line and in the rear were Pitsligo and Kilmarnock's horse on the left, and on the right Elcho and Balmerino's horse (some 360 in all) with the French and Irish troops in the centre with Prince Charles.

Opposite them were the three dragoon regiments of Colonel Ligonier, Cobham and Hamilton and the foot regiments of Wolfe, Cholmondley, Pulteney, the Royals, Price and Ligonier's foot. In the second row were Blackeneys, Munro's, Fleming's, Battereau's and Barrel's foot. Supporting in the rear were the Glasgow volunteers and the Argyll militia. Howard's regiment formed a reserve and Colonel Cunning-ham's artillery played no part, six English cannon being stuck in the mud of Maggie Wood's Loan.

The Battle

Hawley relied on his dragoons. He had

fought with Evans's dragoons at Sheriff-muir and they were the cream of his army as far as he was concerned. Colonel Ligonier was given the order to attack. 'The height of rashness' he thought as his men rode slowly up the steep hill. They broke into a trot and only ten yards from the Macdonald front line they were met by a strong volley as every loaded Scottish musket fired; 80 men fell and almost as many horses. Only some of Lt Col Whitney's dragoons pierced the front rank, but Whitney himself was killed and the Scots fell down and struck out at the horses' legs with their dirks. The survivors fled, many of them through the ranks of the Glasgow militia. The bulk of Cobham's dragoons galloped down the ravine which separated the two armies, fired on as they went by the Jacobite muskets.

The right wing of the Jacobite army swept on in pursuit but the left wing stayed firm. Hawley's second-in-command kept his head and, with Ligonier's foot, Price's and Barrel's regiments, he out-flanked the Scots and prevented the left wing from advancing. Had there been a commander on the left wing—Lord George commanded the right on foot—then the battle of Falkirk might have been a great victory. The Camerons and Stewarts were forced back; Murray brought forward his Atholl men and held back the advancing English infantry as well as Cobham's dragoons who were now re-forming. The rain in the meantime took heavy toll of both English and Scottish firearms—not one in twenty would work. Hawley now ordered a retreat; three of his cannon were dragged off and the rest were captured, together with many of his tents which he had failed to set on fire. Murray entered Falkirk victorious and Lord John Drummond had a skirmish with some Hanoverian troops in the High Street. He was slightly wounded but the town was soon captured. Hawley retreated to Linlithgow and later to Edinburgh where some of his dragoons were hanged in public for their cowardice. Of Hawley's army, about 500 men were killed and 600

taken prisoner, some of the latter being sent to Doune Castle. Colonels Munro, Whitney, Biggar and Powell were killed and poor Ligonier died of pleurisy a few days later. Fifty Jacobites were killed and Lochiel and his brother slightly injured.

The Duke of Cumberland soon took over from Hawley; on 31 January a Jacobite council at Falkirk decided, as many men had gone home with their booty, to march north to Inverness. The forts in Government hands in the north were to be captured and it was planned to wait until the spring when a new army could be gathered and could once more attack the English. Perhaps an all-out attack on Edinburgh would have been more successful. The Scots were never at their best in retreating and an accidental explosion at St Ninian's church, where their ammunition and powder were stored, hastened them on their way. It was a situation similar to Hopton's at Lansdown, but there was to be no Roundway Down to follow it.

Falkirk Today

The battlefield is mostly built over today, but Maggie Wood's Loan can still be found off the Stirling road. There is a monument at the top of the hill erected in 1927, and in the church there is a memorial to young Glengarry, killed by accident by a Highlander who had captured a musket. There is also a monument to Colonel Munro and his brother.

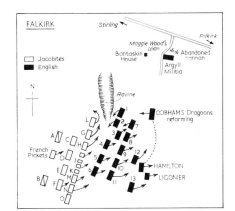

English Army
1 Ligonier (RW)
2 Price
3 Royals
4 Pulteney
5 Cholmondeley
6 Wolfe
7 Barrel
8 Battereau
9 Fleming
10 Munro
11 Blakeney
12 Howard
13 Glasgow Volunteers

Jacobite Army
A Pitsligo
B Elcho
C Drummond
D Gordon
E Ogilvy
F Atholl
G Cameron
H Fraser
J Macintosh
K Farquharson
L Stewart
M Glengarry
N Clanranald
O Keppoch
The Mackintosh company fought side by side with the Macphersons on the left and the Mackenzies on the right

Culloden Moor/16 April 1746

Old Lenach farmhouse, Culloden, now restored as a battle museum (*The National Trust for Scotland*)

The bleakness of Culloden Moor (*The National Trust for Scotland*)

Much has been written about the final battle of The '45. The retreat from Falkirk was seen as a repeat of The '15 by Jacobites in the south, but the Jacobite army was still strong. It succeeded in capturing Fort George at Inverness and blowing it up; Fort Augustus was also captured and Lord George Murray made a raid into Perthshire. Lord Loudon's militia was forced north into Ross-shire and the weather for the time being kept Cumberland from following up their enemies. By the middle of April the weather had cleared and, over 7,000 strong, Cumberland moved up to Nairn. A small force under Lord John Drummond was sent to dispute its passage over the Spey, but at Nairn they found Cumberland's horse outnumbered them so they turned tail and were pursued for two miles. Meanwhile Charles had his headquarters at Culloden House, while his army on the moor had no provisions apart from a ship's biscuit each. It was wet and cold. The Council of War decided on a night attack on Cumberland's camp at Nairn but it was a mad idea; the men were too tired and the van under Murray was separated from the rest with Charles. Before they reached Nairn it was daylight and Murray took the decision to retreat. Charles was infuriated and the army so tired when it returned that many fell soundly asleep in the hedges and fields, while others went to Inverness. Some 2,100 troops were away when the call came for the army to form positions. The Fitzjames horse went to Inverness to round up the stragglers but many men, too tired to move, were cut down by Kingston's horse or rounded up after the battle.

The Jacobite right wing had a walled enclosure which Cumberland's men, the Campbells, were quick to occupy and use as a flank firing position. Murray placed his Atholl men on the right wing where the Macdonalds had traditionally fought and a squabble arose; the Duke of Perth, commanding the left, tried to calm them. The second line was commanded by Colonel Stapleton of the Irish pickets, with the Ogilvy's and Lord John Drummond's regiment. Three four-gun batteries, protected by piles of peat and baskets of mud or clay or positioned behind walls, formed Charles's artillery. The guns were of different calibre and their commander, Finlayson, an Edinburgh mathematician, had little knowledge of warfare.

Brevet-Colonel Belford on the Hanoverian side, however, was a very competent artillery officer. His 9-pounders were equipped to fire grape or ball shot and his artillerymen were experienced gun-handlers. Cumberland's order book for the day still exists; the infantrymen were instructed to thrust their bayonets at the right breast of the enemy so that they would attack his undefended side, for Highlanders carried their targes on their left arm. It was a shrewd move. They were to fire, rear rank first, then centre rank then front rank when the enemy were within ten or twelve paces—such was the unreliability of the musket.

The Battle

The opening cannon fire killed many. The Scots were impatient: Murray urged his left wing to attack but the message never got through to the Macdonalds, the messenger being killed before he could deliver it. The Atholl men were joined by Frasers, Stewarts and Camerons in the centre who were forced to the right in their advance, possibly because they wanted to get out of the line of the Duke's cannon, or because they saw that the Macdonalds were hanging back. On the Duke's left Barrel's Regiment and Munro's (commanded by Dejean) were broken by the onrushing Highlanders but Wolfe's regiment turned and caught them in the flank and the Campbells in the park fired on them in their advance and retreat, cutting them down in great numbers. Some stopped to throw stones, their pistols or muskets, if they had had any, being discarded after one shot. The Macdonalds never reached the enemy. Keppoch made a brave charge alone but was killed. The Irish stood firm and beat back Kingston's horse who tried to get through after the fleeing Macdonalds. On the other wing Lord Mark Kerr's dragoons advanced through behind the wall and threatened the Jacobite's right flank. The few Fitzjames horse kept them at bay for a time but soon the clans were in full retreat to Inverness. O'Sullivan—one of the 'seven men of Moidart'—took the bridle of Prince Charles's horse and led him quickly off the field. Surprisingly almost all the Highland chiefs escaped; Lochiel, wounded in the ankles, was placed on a horse by four Camerons. Murray, the last to leave, seemed to bear a charmed life; he eventually got to Holland but was never forgiven by Charles, whose escape and wanderings in Scotland are part of the legend of that country. Government losses were 364; on the Jacobite side nearly 2,000, mostly killed after the battle.

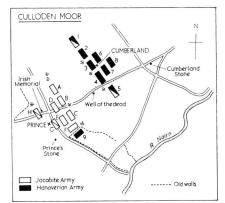

Culloden Today

Leave Inverness by the A9 and turn off on the B9006. The battlefield is National Trust for Scotland property; the clan gravestones mostly date from the nineteenth century. Leanach cottage has some interesting remains and the information centre is a useful spot. Nothing remains of the enclosure walls, and the trees on the moor make the actual positions of the two armies difficult to establish. There is an atmosphere of gloom; the author camped there once—it was April 1975, wet and cold like it must have been 229 years earlier.

Jacobite Army

A Macdonalds and Duke of Perth
B Farquharsons, Macleans, Mackintoshes, Frasers, Stewarts of Appin, Camerons
C Lord George Murray's Atholl Brigade
D Irish under Brigadier Stapleton
E Lord Drummond's Royal Scots, Lord Lewis Gordon
F Ogilvy Regiment
G Fitzjames Horse and Life Guards
H Reserve under Lord Balmerino

Hanoverian Army

1 Cobham's Dragoons, Kingston's Horse
2 Pulteney, Royal Scots
3 Cholmondeley, Price, Royal Scots Fusiliers
4 Munro, Barrel
5 Wolfe
6 Battereau, Howard, Fleming
7 Bligh, Sempill, Ligonier
8 Blakeney
9 Campbells

The Duke of Cumberland with his army crossing the Spey (*Radio Times Hulton Picture Library*)

Fishguard/21/23 February 1797

Trehowel Farm (*author*)

Fishguard 1797 was not, in fact, a battle, yet one British regiment—the Pembroke Yeomanry—is entitled to wear the Fishguard honours on its colours. The strange business of the French landing in Wales in 1797 is often not mentioned in history books; few take it seriously and yet, had it been followed up, Tate's little invasion could have been really serious. At the time of the Naval mutinies at the Nore and Spithead Pitt was, with difficulty, hanging onto a country which jeered him in the streets with cries of 'No bread, no war'; the solitary victory of Howe's 'Glorious First of June' and the English blockade were the only successes in three years.

In France—before Napoleon's rise to power—Carnot was the chief minister. His army under Hoche put down a rising in La Vendee; a triple plan, inspired by Wolfe Tone, was to land troops in Ireland, threaten Newcastle and create a foothold in Wales. The Bantry Bay expedition nearly succeeded, but the weather prevented the French army disembarking in Ireland. General Quantin's second hook of the triple plan was to take a raiding force in fast frigates to Newcastle and burn the docks. A third force under Colonel Tate, an American from Charleston who had been a prisoner of the British during the American War of Independence, was to take the Black Legion and attack Bristol. Later this was changed to Wales and Liverpool.

In the final event, Quantin's fleet suffered damage by storm in Dunkirk harbour. Tate's force of 600 regulars and 800 'convicts' with some Irish officers was equipped with modern flintlock muskets, 5 feet long, with ring-type bayonets and ample supplies of ammunition. Their one weakness was no land transport and insufficient food; Hoche expected them to get both when they landed. For transport they had three fast privateers, *Resistance*, *Constance* and *Vengeance* with an able commander, Castagnier, who was not afraid to take risks.

The English troops in Wales were few. In charge of the local Fishguard Fencibles was Lieutenant Knox, whose men manned a small fort at Fishguard; they wore large 'gaucho' hats and were about 250 in total strength. The Pembroke Militia was at Landguard Fort in Suffolk and the local lords, Milford and Cawdor, had two troops of Yeoman cavalry, about 100 men. There were also some sailors and customs men from an armed cutter in Haverfordwest. It was not a very efficient force to repel an invasion.

The Landing

Visitors to Wales will know that the coastline from Fishguard to Swansea is rocky and uninviting. In mid-winter one would imagine the possibility of a foreign landing to be remote. On 22 February the three ships, with a small lugger *Vautour* accompanying them, arrived off Fishguard. They had attempted to sail up the Bristol Channel but the wind and tide was against them, so Hoche's second landing place—'Cardigan Bay for Liverpool'—was accepted. The Fishguard fort opened fire on them and they beat a hasty retreat. A local sloop captain was captured and he recognised a fellow-Welshman on board the *Vengeance*—Bowen, a dismissed servant of Mr Mortimer of Trehowel captured at sea by the French. He pointed out the rocks of Carregwastad and said he knew a path there; the ship's boats took an advance party ashore and, equipped with ropes, the men made a safe landing. Remarkably the 200 foot cliff presented little problem and only one boat capsized. Fourteen hundred men and two women (wives of soldiers who came as laundrymaids) were safely landed and, led by Bowen, the officers seized Trehowel Farm as their headquarters. Nearby a natural defensive position at Carwnda which stands above the village of Llanwnda was occupied and, although the French ships left early next morning, Tate was in a secure position.

The Battle That Did Not Take Place

The French ships naturally caused panic in Fishguard and many took to the hills. A messenger was sent to Colonel Milford at Picton Castle, arriving at 10.30 p.m. The same man woke up Lord Cawdor whose men were due to parade at Haverfordwest for a funeral next day. A scratch force was organised by Cawdor, with his yeomen cavalry and some sailors with eight small guns in carts; four hundred men set out for Fishguard. En route they met Knox's Fencibles, who had abandoned Fishguard, so that the total was 575 men against 1,400 French. When Cawdor's troops arrived at Goodwick, having flushed some French out of Manorowen on the way, they decided to approach Llanwnda by a narrow path. They climbed the hill in the dark where two hundred French grenadiers, lay waiting for them hidden in rocks. For some unknown reason Cawdor ordered a retreat just before the French position was reached; perhaps he realised he was too late or that his troops were inferior to those of the enemy. The darkness must have influenced him as well.

No battle took place. The French were starving, especially the ex-convicts, some of whom had sailed in chains. They were disappointed at losing their ships so

quickly and many had become very drunk on some Portuguese wine they discovered. Tate realised that his lack of food and transport meant he would not be able to make his men fight; some of them were threatening to give up so that they could get some food. Accordingly a message was sent to Cawdor at Fishguard; a message came back from Cawdor agreeing to their surrender the next day and offering 'consideration to an enemy whose numbers are inferior'.

The bluff succeeded. On the way down to Goodwick Sands next day the rocks were lined with Welshmen, dressed in traditional stovepipe hats and red shawls. Tate's men thought they were the Guards and there was no resistance. The remarkable affair was over.

Fishguard Today

The French surrender was signed at the Royal Oak, a well known local public house. Llanwnda is easily found at the top of the hill and there is a monument on Carregwastad Point and another on Goodwick Sands. A trip should be made to Tenby Museum to see the French arms. For further details of this fascinating and unusual invasion, see *Fishguard Fiasco*, published by Five Arches Press, Tenby.

French muskets used at Fishguard (*author*)

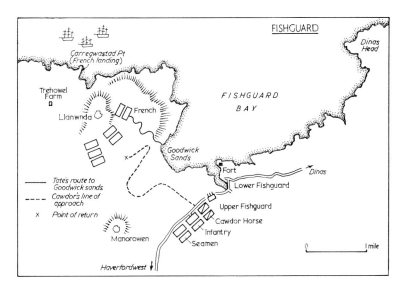

121

Glossary

Some of the words in this book may be unfamiliar to readers. This is an attempt to explain them, but is not intended to be a complete list of military terms:

Arquebus First form of handgun used by Yeomen of the Guard in 1485, fired from the chest.

Artillery Iron pivot guns, called serpentines, firing stone balls of about 4lb weight which were used at Bosworth, Barnet and some other Wars of the Roses battles. In the Civil War the main field guns were:

	Bore	Wt of shot
Falcon	2in	2lb
Minion	3½in	4lb
Saker	3½in	5½lb
Demi-culverin	5½in	9½lb
Culverin	5½in	17lb
Demi-cannon	7in	32lb

By the time of Sedgemoor artillery was no longer manned by infantrymen, but by one gunner and one matross to each gun. Shot could be changed during a battle as at Culloden with devastating effect.

Bayonet A French invention. Bayonets-a-manche or plug-bayonets fitted into the muzzle of a musket (see Killiecrankie) and bayonets-a-douille or socket bayonets were clipped into the side of the musket so that firing could continue.

Bombard Early type of cannon firing stones, sometimes weighing 20lb; usually made of hollow logs with iron bands to prevent splitting and often more dangerous to firer than enemy.

Calthrop (caltrap, caltrop) A three or four-spiked instrument so constructed that one spike is always uppermost. Used by Bruce at Bannockburn and by Warwick at St Albans to obstruct cavalry.

Carabineers Dragoons armed with carbines.

Caracole A cavalry movement (see Edge Hill).

Chamfron Front head armour of a horse.

Arquebusiers

Coehorn mortar Invented by the Dutch General Coehorn in 1672, a small bronze mortar that could throw a 24lb shell 1,200yds. Usually carried in a cart. Effective at Glen Shiel.

Cuirass Jerkin for a soldier consisting of chest and back armour connected by straps, weighing about 16lbs.

Curtal Early type of cannon (see Flodden).

Dragoon Form of mounted infantry. The first real regiment of dragoons was the Scots Greys in 1683, who carried musquetoons on outpost duty. In The '45 dragoon regiments were named after their colonel and were heavily equipped, making them slow on horseback and even slower as infantry. They had ordinary infantry muskets.

Greaves Leg armour.

Hackbut Heavy handgun with butt and serpentine lock, thus a 'hooked-butt' becoming hackbut in the reign of Henry VIII.

Halberd Infantry weapon, commonly used on sentry duty in place of the pike. Many different varieties:

Partisan

Halberd or Bill

Glaive

Poleaxe

Lochaber axe   A long-bladed poleaxe used by the Highlanders in The '15 and The '45. There is one in the Tower of London, supposed to have been used to kill the unfortunate Colonel Gardiner at Prestonpans.

Mace   Used by horsemen from the eleventh to fifteenth centuries for crushing armour. Many different varieties:

Mace   Battleaxe   Morning-star   Battle hammer

Morion   Type of helmet common in Elizabethan era.

Musket   The first muskets were matchlocks fired by a burning match applied to a touch hole; later they were fitted with a lock bringing the match to the priming-pan on trigger release. Then evolved the wheel-lock, invented in Nuremberg in 1517, which had a steel rasped wheel protruding into the pan. The lock was wound up with a key and iron pyrites on the wheel produced a spark. Flintlocks were similar. Later versions used powder, percussion caps or wafers and were more reliable; they were called percussion-lock muskets.

Musquetoon   Type of blunderbus.

Partisan   See *Halberd*.

Pavise   A shield for the whole body that could be stuck in the ground; used at St Albans.

Petard   A container of inflammable material thrown in the way of an advancing enemy or used for blowing up castle gates, etc. The thrower was the petardier.

Peterara   Stone-firing gun. In the fourteenth century a breech-loading peterara was developed that could be fitted to a ship.

Quarrel   Shot bolt or arrow fired from a crossbow.

Sabaton   Armoured shoes worn by knights.

Schiltron   A wedge formation used by Scottish spearmen so that the maximum use of their spears would be made on all flanks; it could be used for either attack or defence (see Bannockburn).

Spontoon   Type of halberd used more for lining up the ranks than for fighting, carried by junior officers and NCOs in the ranks at Culloden.

Swords   Probably the earliest form of weapon after the axe. In the Scottish wars the two-handed sword—the claymore—was used by the Scots with devastating effect at close quarters. Later in The '15 and The '45 they used basket swords with blades on both sides, unlike the English infantry who used short back-swords with only one blade.

Targe   Circular Scottish shield made of wood and hide with metal studs. It was useless against short range musket fire.

Flintlock musket, 1725
(*National Army Museum*)

A breech-loading wheel-lock pistol with ivory stock

Appendix

The Officers of the Cameron Clan

Donald Cameron of Lochiel, Chief and Colonel

Alexander Cameron of Dungallon, Major

Alexander Cameron of Dungallon, son of above, Standard Bearer

Alexander Cameron of Druimnasallie

Alexander Cameron, brother of Lochiel, Priest

Alexander Cameron of Glennevis

Allan Cameron of Lundavra, Lieutenant

Allan Cameron of Callart, Lieutenant

Allan Cameron, brother of Glennevis

Archibald Cameron, Doctor, brother of Lochiel and ADC to Prince Charles

Donald Cameron of Erracht

Donald Cameron of Glenpean

Duncan Cameron, Fortinghall, Episcopal chaplain

Duncan Cameron, Nine Mile Water

Ewen Cameron of Inverlochy, Captain

Ewen Cameron of Dawnie, Captain

Ewen Cameron, uncle of Callart

Ewen Cameron, brother of Druimnasallie

Ewen Cameron of Annock

James Cameron, Ensign

John Cameron, brother of Callart

Ludovic Cameron of Torcastle, uncle of Lochiel

Cameron of Arroch, Captain

Cameron of Clunes

Cameron of Kinlochleven

Cameron of Strone

John Cameron, Presbyterian Minister of Fort William

Clan Cameron Casualties after Culloden

Donald Cameron of Lochiel: Wounded in the legs, but escaped to France on *Le Conti* in September 1746; Died at Borgue, France, in 1748

Allan Cameron of Lundavra, Lieutenant Killed Prestonpans

James Cameron, Ensign: Killed Prestonpans

Allan Cameron of Clunes: Killed Prestonpans

Allan Cameron of Glennevis: Killed Culloden

Alexander Cameron of Strone: Wounded Culloden

Cameron of Corrychurichan: Wounded Culloden

Ewen MacMillan of Murlaggan: Killed Culloden

John MacMillan of Murlaggan: Killed after Culloden

Others: 4 died in prison, 3 executed, 4 banished, 23 transported to the colonies (including 3 women), 19 released after some imprisonment and the fate of 8 prisoners unknown.

Alexander Cameron, the Priest, brother of Lochiel was captured and died on board a prison ship. Ludovic Cameron of Torcastle was attained but escaped to France. Dr Archibald Cameron escaped to France but was sent back twice to Scotland, where he had knowledge of secret Jacobite funds buried at Lockarkaig. He was betrayed on his second trip in 1753, captured, tried and hanged at Tyburn. He was buried at the Savoy Chapel, where there is a Victorian monument to him.

Bibliography

Apart from pamphlets, anonymous books on special battles like that on *Sheriffmuir* of 1898, and many booklets and documents used as reference material, the following general works were of use and should be consulted for further reading.

Barnett, C., *Britain and her Army*, Allen Lane, 1970

Brooke, H., *Visits to Fields of Battle in England*, Russell Smith, 1857 (reissued by Sutton 1975)

Burne, A. H., *Battlefields of England*, Methuen, 1952

—— *More Battlefields of England*, Methuen, 1952

Coate, Mary, *Cornwall in the Civil War*, Bradford Barton, 1965

Elcho, Lord, *The Affairs of Scotland* 1744, 1745, 1746, reissued by the Mercat Press, 1973

Gardiner, S. R., *History of the Great Civil War*, Vols I–IV, Longmans, 1901

Grant, J., *British Battles at Land and Sea*, Cassell, 1890

Hume Brown, P., *History of Scotland*, Vols I–III, Cambridge, 1901

Kemp, H., *The Jacobite Rebellion*, Almark, 1975

Kinross, John, *Fishguard Fiasco*, Five Arches Press, 1974

—— *Discovering Battlefields of England*, Shire Publications, 1974

—— *Discovering Battlefields of Scotland*, Shire Publications, 1976

Lang, A., *History of Scotland*, Vols I–IV, Blackwood, 1902

McCoy, G. A. Hayes, *Irish Battles*, Longman, 1969

Montgomery of Alamein, Field Marshal Viscount, *A History of Warfare*, Collins, 1968

Robson, James, *Border Battles and Battlefields*, Rutherford, 1897

Rogers, Col. H. C. B., *Battles and Generals of the Civil War*, Seeley Service, 1968

Ross, C., *The Wars of the Roses*, Thames & Hudson, 1976

Seymour, W., *Battles in Britain*, Vols I–II, Sidgwick & Jackson, 1975

Stewart, J., *The Camerons—A History of the Clan Cameron*, Clan Cameron Assoc, Stirling, 1974

Thomasson, K., and Buist, F., *Battles of The '45*, Batsford, 1962

Tayler, A. & H., *1715. The Story of a Rising*, Edinburgh, 1936

Taylor, W., *The Military Roads of Scotland*, David & Charles, 1976

Warner, P., *British Battlefields*, Vols I–IV, Osprey, 1973

Williams, D. T., *The Battle of Bosworth*, Leicester University Press, 1975

Woolrych, A., *Battles of the English Civil War*, Batsford, 1961

Young, Brigadier P., *Edgehill*, Roundwood Press, 1968

—— *Marston Moor*, Roundwood Press, 1970

Index

Gardiner, Colonel, 112, 113, 123
George I, King, 106
George II, King, 113
George, Prince of Denmark, 102
Gerard, Colonel Charles, 72
Glasgow Volunteers, 116, 117
Glendower, Owen, 28
Glenham, Sir Thomas, 77
Glengarry Regiment, 115
Gloucester, Duke of, 22, 23
Gloucester, Gilbert, Earl of, 18, 20, 21
Gloucester, Richard, see Richard III
Gloucester, Robert, Earl of, 17
Gordon, Adam, 29
Gordon, General, 106
Gordon, Lewis, Lord, 83, 86, 87
Gordon, Nathaniel, 87
Goring, George, Baron, 76, 77, 78, 80
Grafton's Horse, 97
Graham, James, see Montrose, Marquis of
Gray, Sir Thomas, 22, 23
Grenville, Sir Bevil, 64, 66, 67, 68, 69
Grey, Lord of Ruthin, 33
Grey, Lord of Wilton, 56, 57
Grey, Lord, 96, 97, 98
Guards, 1st and 2nd, 97
Gustavus Adolphus, King, of Sweden, 58, 61
Guthrun, King of the Danes, 10, 11

Hamilton's Dragoons, 112, 116
Hamilton, 1st Duke of, 90, 91
Hamilton, General, 106, 107
Hamilton, James, Earl of Arran, 90, 91
Hamilton, Richard, 102, 103
Hammond, Colonel, 84
Hampden, John, 62
Hardrada, King of Norway, 12
Harold, King, 12–15
Harrington, Sir James, 42
Hastings, William, Baron, 42, 43, 44, 45
Hawley, General, 112, 113, 116, 117
Henry, Prince of Scotland, 17
Henry III, King, 18, 19, 20, 21, 32
Henry IV, King, 28, 32, 33
Henry V, King, 37
Henry VI, King, 37, 40, 41, 42
Henry VII, King, 37, 46, 48, 51
Henry VIII, King, 37, 50, 53, 54, 56
Hepburn, Sir Patrick, Younger of Hailes, 28
Heron, John, 52
Hertford, Earl of, 54
Hertford, Marquis of, 68, 70
Heselrig, Sir Arthur, 68, 70, 71, 93
Hesse, Prince of, 102
Hobart's Horse, 72
Hoche, General, 120
Holmes, 97
Home, Earl of, 50, 51, 52, 56, 57
Honeywood, Colonel, 115
Hope, Lord, son of, 58
Hopton, Sir Ralph, 64, 66, 68, 69, 70
'Hotspur', Henry Percy, 28, 29
Houghton's House, Preston, 105
Howard, Sir Edmund, 50, 52, 53
Howard, Thomas, Admiral of England, 50, 51, 53
Howard, Colonel Thomas, 84
Howard, Thomas, Earl of Norfolk, 46
Howard, Thomas, Earl of Surrey, 46, 50, 53
Howard's Regiment, 116
Howe, Admiral, 120
Huffel, Colonel, 109

Hungerford, Walter, 46
Huntley's Highlanders, 50, 51, 52
Hurry, Colonel John, 80, 82, 83

Ireton's Horse, 84

James II, King, 96, 97, 98, 100, 102, 103
James IV, King, 50, 51, 52, 53
James VIII, King, 106, 107, 108, 110
Jeffreys, Judge, 98
John, Bishop of Chichester, 18
John, King of France, 26
Johnstone, Chevalier, 113
Jones, Captain, 98

Keith, George, see Earl Marischal
Keith, James, 108, 109
Keith, Sir Robert, 22, 23
Keith, Sir William, 24
Kenmure, Lord, 104, 105
Kerr, Colonel George, 115
Kerr, Lord Mark, 119
Kerr's Dragoons, 107
Kilmarnock, Countess of, 116
Kilmarnock's Horse, 116
Kilpont, Lord, 82
King, Colonel, 72
King, James, 50
King's Horse Guards, 97
King's Regiment of Horse, 97
Kingston's Horse, 118
Kiriel, Sir Thomas, 40
Kirke's 'Lambs', 97
Knox, John, 56
Knox, Lieut, 120

Lambert, General John, 76, 90, 94
Langdale, Sir Marmaduke, 76, 90, 91
Latour, Sir Brian, 54, 55
Laud, Archbishop, 58
Lauzun, Count, 102, 103
Lawers Campbells, 83
Le Gros, William, 17
Lennox, Earl of, 52, 53
Leslie, General Sir Alexander, 58, 59, 76, 88, 89, 92, 93, 94
Leslie, Norman, Master of Rothes, 54
Leven, Earl of, see Leslie, General
Ligonier, Colonel, 116, 117
Lilburn, Colonel Henry, 94
Lincoln, Robert, Earl of, 48, 49
Lindsay, Lord, 86
Lindsey, Earl of, 61
Lisle, Sir George, 80, 81
Livingstone, Master of, 57
Lothian Regiment, 83
Loudon, Lord, 118
Loudon's Foot, 83
Loughborough, Lord, 72
Louis IX, King, 18
Louis XII, King, 50
Louis XIV, King, 106
Lucy, Sir Thomas, 26, 105
Lunsford, Colonel, 58

Macdonalds, 82, 100, 118, 119
Macdonald, Alasdair, 83
Macdonald of Clanranald, 116
Macdonald of Glengarry, 116
Macdonald of Keppoch, 112, 116
Macdonells, 100
Macdowall, 28
Macgregors, 108
Mackay, General, 100, 101
Mackenzies, 108, 116
Mackintosh, Brigadier, 104
Mackintosh of Mackintosh, 105
Maclachlans, 113
MacLeans, 107

Macleod of Assynt, 89
Macpherson, Cluny, 115
Macraes, 107, 108
Macrae-Gilstrap, Colonel, 109
Manchester, Edward Montagu, 2nd Earl of, 80, 81
Mar, Earl of, 104, 106, 107
March, Edward, Earl of, see Edward IV
Margaret, Queen, 30, 31, 33, 34, 35, 38, 39, 40, 41, 42, 43, 44, 45
Mary, Queen, 98
Mary, Queen of Scots, 56
Massey, Colonel Edward, 94
Matilda, 16
Matthews, 97
Maurice, Prince, 68, 70, 71, 74, 78, 80, 81
McLeods, 112
Meldrum, Sir John, 61, 72, 73
Menteith, Sir John, Governor of Dunbarton, 22
Menteith Militia, 106
Merrick, Sir John, 79
Mewtas, Sir Peter, 57
Middleton, Sir Thomas, 75, 78, 79, 90
Milford, Lord, 120, 121
Millar, Captain, 104
Modena, Mary of, 108
Mohun, Lord, 64, 78
Molyneux, Sir William, 53
Monmouth, Duke of, 96, 97, 98, 99
Monroes, 109
Monro, Sir George, 90, 91
Montagu, Colonel, 109
Montagu, John, Marquis of, 42
Monteagle, Lord, see Stanley, Sir Edward
Montgomery, General, 95
Montrose, Earl of, 52, 53
Montrose, Marquis of, 59, 82, 83, 86, 87, 88, 89, 90, 92
Moray, Earl of, 29
Moray, Randolph, Earl of, 22, 23
Moray Horse, 83
Morcar, King Harold's brother-in-law, 12
Mortimer, Anne, 37
Mortimer, Roger, 20, 21
Mortimer, Mr, of Trehowel, 120
Mowbray, Governor of Stirling Castle, 22, 23
Monro, Colonel, 117
Murray, Lord Charles, 104
Murray, Lord George, 83, 108, 109, 112, 113, 114, 115, 116, 118, 119

Napier, Master of, 86
Neville, Lord, of Raby Castle, 26
Newcastle, Marquis of, 72, 76, 77
Nithsdale, Viscount, 104
Norfolk, John, Duke of, 26, 41
Norfolk, Thomas Howard, Earl of, 46
Northampton, Earl of, 75
Northern Levies, 83
Northumberland, Henry, Earl of, 41, 46, 47

Ogilvy, Master of, 57
Ogilvy's Regiment, 118, 119
Oglethorpe, Colonel, 97, 98
Okey, Colonel John, 84, 85
Olaf, 13
O'Neill, Sir Neill, 103
Ormonde, Duke of, 102, 106, 108
O'Sullivan, John William, 119
Oxburgh, Colonel, 105
Oxford, Earl of, 102
Oxford, John de Vere, 13th Earl, 42, 43, 46, 48, 49